GUILTY or INNOCENT?

The Cormack Brothers
– trial, execution and exhumation

Nancy Murphy

Published by

Published in 1998 by
RELAY BOOKS
Tyone, Nenagh, Co. Tipperary
Tel/Fax: (067) 31734

ISBN 0 946327 20 3

British Library Cataloguing-in-Publication Data
A catalogue record for this book is available from the British Library

*This book is published
with the support of Tipperary Leader Group*

Design and typesetting: in-house by RELAY
Typeface: Times, 11.5 on 12.5
Pages size: 216 x 156 mm

Printed by Nenagh Guardian Ltd. on 90gr matt art

We never make mistakes.

– Alexander Solzhenitsyn,
An Incident at
Krechetovka Station (1963)

Acknowledgements

Several people and repositories have contributed directly and indirectly to the compilation of this book and I acknowledge their assistance. Firstly, I am grateful to the National Archives, National Library of Ireland, Nenagh Guardian Ltd (especially Patrick A. Ryan), Tipperary County Library (especially Mary Guinan Darmody, Local Studies Section), Tipperary North Family History Foundation (especially Nora O'Meara), the Valuation Office, and John G. Walsh, Templemore, for access to, and permission to quote from the records in their possession. Thanks are also due to John Joe Buckley, D.C.C., and Aileen Quigley of the District Court office, Nenagh, and Matt Hassett and Maura Ryan of James O'Brien & Co., Nenagh, for access to statutes and legal texts; to Patrick J. Ryan, Oldbawn, Loughmore, who first discovered the valuable Samuel Cooke letters and who advised me on the Cormack genealogy; to Michael Maher, Leugh, for information on James Maher. I am also grateful for the help given me by Very Rev. Maurice Dooley, P.P., Loughmore-Castleiny, who put parish records, documents and maps at my disposal, took photographs on request and translated the Latin inscriptions on the plaques.

Finally, I am especially indebted to Daniel Grace for reading the various drafts, correcting errors, and making numerous helpful suggestions; to Elaine Burke Houlihan of RELAY for typesetting, proof reading and correcting, and for her incisive suggestions; to Donal A. Murphy for specialist research and overall editing unstintingly given; to Kevin Walshe, graphic artist, who designed the cover, and Nenagh Guardian Ltd who were responsible for the book's printing and binding.

The photographs listed on the pages below are courtesy of the following: Lawrence Collection, NLI, viii, 41; Dermot Cahill, S.E.C.B. Soc., Dovea, 128; Very Rev. Maurice Dooley, 7, 9, 157; Matt Hassett, James O'Brien & Co., Solrs, Nenagh,131; Martin Maher, Co. Librarian, 134 & 150 (by E. Shanahan, stationer, Thurles), 145 & 148 (by P.J.R.); Donal A. Murphy, 24, 33; Brendan Treacy, Nenagh (Lewy Gleeson collection),133, 146, 147.

Nancy Murphy, a regional historian based in Nenagh, is a native of Drom-Inch which adjoins Loughmore parish. She has had articles on diverse local history topics published in journals and anthologies and is a regular contributor to the 'From Script and Stone' series in The Guardian. *She is author of* Walkabout Nenagh *(1994) and* A Trip Through Tipperary Lakeside *(1997). She is a founder member and officer of the Ormond Historical Society, Nenagh District Heritage Society and Tipperary North Family History Foundation.*

Contents

Abbreviations

CSORP	Chief Secretary's Office Registered Papers
DEP	*Dublin Evening Post*
FJ	*Freeman's Journal*
Grace, *Portrait of a Parish*	Daniel Grace, *Portrait of a Parish: Monsea and Killodiernan* (Nenagh 1996).
Kenny's *Outlines*	J.W. Cecil Turner ed., Kenny's *Outlines of Criminal Law,* 19th edition (Cambridge 1966).
LR & TV	*Limerick Reporter and Tipperary Vindicator*
Murphy, *Two Tipperarys*	Donal A. Murphy, *The Two Tipperarys* (Nenagh 1994).
NA	National Archives
NG	*Nenagh Guardian*
NLI	National Library of Ireland
NN & TV	*Nenagh News and Tipperary Vindicator*
O'Connor, *The Irish Justice*	James O'Connor, *The Irish Justice of the Peace*, 2nd edition (Dublin 1915), vols. i & ii.
TS	*Tipperary Star*

Errata

p. 31:	'1952' should read '1852'.
p. 80, third paragraph:	'entirely … on either of them' should read 'or either of them'.
p. 105:	last sentence of 5th par should read – 'He re-affirmed his belief in the inviolability …'
p. 107:	'William Leahy' should read 'Patrick Leahy'.
pp. 10, 12, 18, 32, 57, 69:	'Castleiney' should be 'Castleiny'.

Introduction

The story of the Cormack Brothers is one that has lived on in the folk memory, not only in County Tipperary and Ireland but in England, Canada, America and Australia. In Ireland it has been adapted for the stage, both as straight drama and as a musical, for a radio documentary and as a novel. It has been told, in so far as it was known, in newspaper articles and local publications. The most extensive of these was the series in *An Droichead* by Patrick J. Ryan, Loughmore, who, like myself, has been interested in the story longer than we care to remember.

I first heard of the Cormacks over fifty years ago when my mother recounted the story of how our neighbour, William Purcell, Lissaroon in the parish of Drom-Inch, had gone to the funeral in his ass and car. In later years I saw the Cormack mausoleum in Loughmore and John Ellis's grave in Killahara graveyard.

In Nenagh the former gaol entrance is inextricably linked with the execution of the Cormack Brothers. When the former gaol Governor's House was converted to a heritage centre in 1983-4 the exhibitions included the history of the building and touched on the story of the Cormacks. In the course of researching this I made the acquaintance of the late Paul Walsh, Templemore, who gave me copies of his father John's papers relating to the Cormacks' funeral in 1910. When these were put with the content of the file which had been donated by Michael Black, solicitor, of James O'Brien & Co., Nenagh, to the Co. Library, Thurles, the full story of the exhumation and re-burial unfolded.

In the 1980s the upper floor of the former gaol gatehouse had reached a derelict state and was inaccessible. The Heritage Society, in conjunction with the Sisters of Mercy, devised a restoration plan. For the first time there were revealed to the public the exercise yards, day rooms, condemned cells, 'execution room', holes for scaffold timbers and iron fittings. It was a fitting place to tell the story of the Cormacks, albeit in brief.

After fifteen years of sporadic research, *Guilty or Innocent?* is an expansion of that story.

The numerous people who appear in it are all now gone to their eternal reward. I will conclude with the final words of the death sentence: May the Lord have mercy on their souls.

The entrance to the County Gaol, circa 1910. The statue is in front of the doors
which opened inwards to give access to the scaffold.

Chapter 1
'Boys, we are dying innocent'

On the eleventh of May in '58 the hanging it took place
And by a holy Pastor they were both reconciled to grace;
Such thunder, rain and lightning has not been witnesssed since,
As the Lord above sent down from Heaven as a token of their innocence.

Sixteen years had elapsed since the local populace first witnessed such a scene, and it was nine years previously since a human life was publicly terminated in this ignoble way and on that spot – outside Tipperary North Riding's County Gaol at Nenagh.

A crowd of onlookers had gathered on this fine Tuesday morning in May to witness the spectacle. As the scaffold was sited at first-floor level their view was not impeded by the three lines of police, some mounted on horseback, who occupied the roadway in front of the gaol entrance.

The hangman had already emerged to grease the ropes and check the scaffold's mechanical parts. He wore a flannel shirt, with sleeves tucked up; his head was covered by a black serge veil.

The two prisoners, aware since Saturday that petitions for a reprieve of their sentence had failed, attended an early morning Mass and received Holy Communion.

At 11 o'clock the sub-Sheriff of County Tipperary arrived with the death warrant.

The prisoners were taken from their individual cells to the preparatory 'execution room'. The sub-Sheriff, prison staff, gaol chaplain and other Nenagh parish clergy accompanied them. The preparation room was directly behind and only a few paces from the scaffold. The wrists and arms of the condemned men were tightly bound behind their backs by the hangman.

The silent crowd waiting below, heads uncovered and kneeling, saw the glazed doors behind the scaffold open inwards. Both prisoners stepped on to the platform of the scaffold, with its twin trapdoors of hinged leaves held in position from below by bolts.

Each prisoner was accompanied by a priest holding a crucifix. The small group were reciting the Litany of Jesus.

The crowd saw two fresh-complexioned young men of medium height, one brown-haired, one fair. The fact that they were brothers added to the poignancy of the scene. Relatives and acquaintances present could see that the fair one stood tall and looked strong; the other appeared thin and leaned on the priest for support.

Each young man in turn took a step or two forward on the platform and spoke to the assembled police and crowd.

'Lord have mercy on me, for you, oh Jesus, know that I had neither hand, act nor part for which I am about to die. Good people, pray for me. Lord have mercy on me.'

'Boys, we are dying innocent. Lord have mercy on us. We had neither hand, act nor part in the murder of Ellis'.

The hangman stepped forward, positioned each man on the trapdoors, placed a white cloth over the head and face of each, and a rope noose around each neck. The knot was drawn tight on each prisoner's left jaw and held in position by a sliding ring.

The time was 11.30 a.m.

A quick shift of a lever by the hangman withdrew the bolts which held each trapdoor closed. When each body reached the end of the drop allowed by the length of the rope, a jerk reaction broke or dislocated the first three cervical vertebrae and so damaged the vital part of the spinal cord, causing instantaneous unconsciousness.

Within seconds the bodies of William and Daniel Cormack hung suspended above the lines of silent police and crowd.

Chapter 2
'The almost perfectly tranquil state'

That public hanging on Tuesday 11 May 1858 of William and Daniel Cormack, pronounced guilty of the murder of John Ellis, was to be the last of such scenes in Nenagh.

The hanging in 1842 of James Smith alias Shea, Cloughjordan, was the first, Smith having been found guilty of murder.[1]

Over the next seven years a further fourteen men were to face the hangman in the preparatory 'execution room'[2] and stand on the trapdoors. The last of those was 26-year-old John Tierney from the parish of Drom near Templemore.[3]

The fifteen persons executed before William and Daniel Cormack included two sets of brothers: Thomas and John Wade, Kilcommon, Thurles, and John and Michael Connolly, Moyne, Thurles.[4]

The following is the full list of persons executed prior to 1858:[5]

James Smith alias Shea (24)	1842	murder of Rody Kennedy, farmer, Laughane, Cloughjordan.
Michael Moylan (22)	1843	murder of John Nolan, herdsman, Ballinakill, Roscrea.
John Cooke (20)	1844	ditto.
John Hickey (35)	1844	murder of Michael Hanley, farmer, Greenhall, Newport.
Thomas Wade (25)	1844	murder of Patrick Ryan (Morgan), farmer, Kilcommon, Thurles.
John Wade (28)	1844	ditto.
Patrick Rice (20)	1846	murder of Patrick Clarke, landlord, Southill, Nenagh.
Patrick Hayes (20)	1846	ditto.
William Fogarty (25)	1846	shooting at Michael McDonald, slate quarry manager, Castletownarra, Portroe.
William Walsh (30)	1846	murder of Daniel Birachree, Toureenbrien, Newport.
John Connolly (26)	1847	murder of Thomas Dillon, process server, Moyne, Thurles.

Michael Connolly (25)	1847	murder of Thomas Dillon, Moyne.
James Carthy (21)	1848	conspiracy to murder R.U. Bayly, land agent, Ballinaclough, Nenagh.
Martin Ryan (26)	1848	shooting at Robert Lloyd, landlord, Longfordwood Hse, Templemore.
John Tierney (26)	1849	murder of Thomas Burke, tailor, Drom, Templemore.

PATTERNS

Murders, or attempted murders, committed in the riding in the year 1850 averaged four every three months. The victims were Pat Shanahan, Brittas, Thurles; William Ardill, steward to Richard Falkiner, Mount Falcon, near Borrisokane; Thomas Martin, Clonmore, Templemore; Michael Dunphy, Coolkennedy, Thurles; James Atkinson, Borrisokane; William Hogan, Toomevara, Nenagh; William Gleeson, Shallee, Nenagh; Michael Kennedy, Nenagh; John O'Shea, Newport; Judith Murphy, Littleton, Thurles; Patrick Ryan, Gortshane, Newport; Patrick Cleary, Riverlawn, Ballymackey near Nenagh. There were unsuccessful attempts made on the lives of William Kennedy, Bawn, and Francis Kiernan, Loughourna, both in the Nenagh area, Michael McGrath, Newport, and John Cantwell, Roscrea.[6]

The following years, the aftermath of the Great Famine, saw an overall reduction in crime in Tipperary North Riding, as it did throughout Co. Tipperary at large and Ireland as a whole.[7] However, violence against persons was still employed during the 1850s as a means of redress for real or perceived grievances, some relating to evictions and other disputes over land, and some of a personal nature. This category of crime fell throughout the decade more or less in line with the overall reduction.[8]

The incidence of homicide within that same category of crime, described as 'offences against the person with violence', decreased in the riding in the years 1851 to 1857. Extra police were withdrawn from the area in 1852.[9] Criminal cases at the spring and summer assizes in that period were disposed of in one to two days; they had taken ten to fourteen days in the previous decade. Capital punishment was pronounced in only one instance. That was in March 1855 when Michael Hogan and Thady Ryan were sentenced to death for the murder of Denis Moloney in Nenagh the previous August. But on the day appointed for their execution they were preparing to leave the country, having had their sentences commuted to transportation for life. It was a fairly gruesome murder, the young man having been beaten to death. Hogan and Ryan were two of ten persons charged; the others received gaol sentences of varying duration.[10]

At the spring assizes of 1857, Judge William Nicholas Keogh, making his first appearance in Nenagh courthouse since his elevation to the bench the previous year, said in his opening remarks to the grand jury: 'I am happy to be able to congratulate you on the almost perfectly tranquil state of this county …' Of the two murder cases scheduled for hearing, one was postponed and the other accorded a verdict of manslaughter for which two persons were sentenced to four years penal servitude.[11]

Keogh also presided at the 1857 summer assizes. He sentenced Rowan Cashel, gentleman, from the vicinity of Nenagh, to two years imprisonment with hard labour. Cashel and three others had been found guilty of a particularly vicious assault on a Denis O'Brien in Nenagh in early July. The others got twelve months imprisonment each.[12]

It is in this context of an ongoing, though reducing, incidence of violent crime in North Tipperary, and of the variable sentences meted out to those involved, that one places the murder of John Ellis and the subsequent trial and execution of William and Daniel Cormack.

The fact that the Cormacks were the last people to be executed in Nenagh; the public awareness of their case brought about by the very extensive press coverage of their trial and by later agitation; their own repeated declarations of innocence, even on the scaffold – all contributed to the preservation in folk memory of their story, above that of any of the other fifteen. The final factor in heightened public interest was the re-burial of their exhumed remains in 1910.

NOTES
1   *Nenagh Guardian* (*NG* hereafter), 20 Aug 1842.
2   The name 'Execution Room' is still preserved in its original state on the door in the former gaol gatehouse which is now part of Nenagh District Heritage Centre.
3   *NG*, 12 Sept 1849. On the night before the execution Tierney made a declaration of his own guilt and exonerated the two other persons charged with him and also confined in the gaol.
4   *NG*, 25 May 1844. *NG*, 26 April 1848 – the mother and two other brothers of the Connollys were also sentenced to death at a later assizes but were fortunate to be reprieved by the Lord Lieutenant. They were transported to Tasmania.
5   *NG*, 4 Oct 1843, 18 May 1844, 20 June 1846; *Limerick Reporter & Tipperary Vindicator* (*LR & TV* hereafter) 26 Aug 1848; *NG*, 20 Oct 1848; *NG*, 12 May 1858. James Carthy was the second person to be hanged for the R.U. Bayly attack. A James Daily had been tried earlier in the year at a special commission or court in Clonmel and executed there – *NG*, 8 Mar 1848. Bayly, who survived his wounds, made a plea for Carthy's life.
6   *NG,* 12, 25 Jan, 16, 27 Mar, 22, 29 May, 29 June, 27 July, 17 Aug, 9, 20, 23 Oct, 20 Nov, 11 Dec 1850.

7   Annual Reports of the Inspectors-General of Prisons of Ireland; James W. Hurst, 'Disturbed Tipperary: 1831-1860' in *Éire-Ireland*, Fomhar, 1974, appendix A, p. 55. Hurst's main finding was that the overall rate of crime, as measured by committals for trial for all classes of offences, was higher in Tipperary than that in Ireland as a whole. One reflection of this appears in Schedule A to the Constabulary Act, 1848. Tipperary, though approximately equal in population to Galway and having hardly three-quarters the population of Cork, was allocated 1,030 police constables, as against Galway's 704 and Cork's 612. Tipperary's crime rate was approximately double that of Ireland's during the Great Famine and immediate aftermath. It was approximately 150 per cent of Ireland's as a whole from 1853 to 1858 and more or less levelled off in 1859 and 1860 – see his appendix D, p. 58, and graph on p. 59.

8   Hurst, as above, appendix C, p. 57.

9   *NG*, 17 Mar 1852.

10   *NG*, 2 May 1855.

11   *NG*, 14 Mar 1857.

12   *NG*, 29 July 1857.

Chapter 3
Ellis and the Cormacks

John Ellis, a native of Scotland, a married man with five children, was shot dead on the night of Thursday 22 October 1857 as he was being driven home in a horse and car from Templemore railway station by his manservant, 17-year-old Thomas Burke. He had travelled to Dublin the previous evening for the cattle market, as was his regular practice. The incident occurred shortly before midnight in the townland of Kilkillahara, about 260 yards down a narrow bye-road off the main Templemore-Thurles road. The bye-road leads to Dovea village, a further 1.2 miles on.[1]

Ellis was born in 1802 in Fortfarshire, Scotland. He had been agent and farm manager to John Trant, Dovea House, for over twenty-five years.[2] In the Primary Valuation of 1850 he is listed as occupier of Kilrush House (below) valued at £14. However, he is not returned as an occupier of any land in that record.[3]

In January 1852 Ellis purchased 107 acres in Tinvoher townland from the Incumbered Estates Commissioners for £820. The land was part of the extensive estate sold on behalf of the 'Trustees of the late George Goold, Bart., & Henry Valentine Goold and others in Counties Cork and Tipperary'.[4] Ellis is returned as a ratepayer for the land, plus three workmen's houses, in Tinvoher until 1857. In 1858 his name is crossed out and that of William Connolly pencilled in.[5]

In 1854 John Ellis became a tenant of 64 acres 1 rood 35 perches in Clondoty townland. The holding included a cottier's house let to a Michael Moloney.[6] The whole of Clondoty townland (428 acres) had been purchased by John Trant from Sir John Craven Carden, Templemore, in the Incumbered Estates Courts in December 1853. The prospectus for the sale shows that the 64 odd acres which Ellis took on were farmed by Carden himself.[7] Some time after Ellis's death this holding was tenanted in three separate smallholdings.[8]

For about eighteen months before his death Ellis was occupier of 21 acres of the townland of Ballybristy. The holding had two houses tenanted by James Lahey and William Egan. By 1860 the Ellis holding had a new tenant, Laurence Gleeson.[9]

John Gore Jones, Resident Magistrate, Thurles, when reporting the murder to Dublin Castle, described Ellis as 'a skilled agriculturist' and that 'he had purchased a nice property … paid his workmen liberally and was a gentleman in all his dealings'.[10]

In his capacity as John Trant's agent, Ellis would deal with the year-to-year tenants and recommend, if not actually make, the decision on the non-renewal of a tenancy. This might be because a tenant was unsatisfactory or because a prudent farm manager might decide to discontinue letting a particular farm and bring it back under his own management with the rest of the landlord's untenanted land. Putting a new tenant into a farm from which a sitting tenant had been removed put the life of landlord, agent, and new tenant at enormous risk.

At least two unsuccessful attempts were made on Ellis's life prior to October 1857. In May 1849 the Government's reward of £80 for the 'apprehension of the fellow who fired on John Ellis', brought no positive results.[11] The following March the *Nenagh Guardian* reported:

As Mr Ellis, steward to John Trant, Esq., Dovea, was returning from church, accompanied by his wife, child and William Bell, a ploughman to Mr Trant, he was fired at by a ruffian who was standing on a ditch by the roadside at Leugh. The car on which Mr Ellis was seated happened to be going rapidly at the time the

ERECTED
BY ANNE ELLIS
IN MEMORY OF
HER BELOVED HUSBAND
JOHN ELLIS
NATIVE OF FORTFARSHIRE
SCOTLAND
DIED 22 OCTOBER 1857
AGED 55 YEARS
ALSO
WILLIAM ELLIS
DIED 14 JANUARY 1854
AGED 5 MONTHS.

shot was fired and providentially none of the party received the least injury. The police were immediately at the scene of outrage but did not succeed in arresting the villain.

Mr Ellis has stated that he has become obnoxious for having cultivated, tilled and farmed a large tract of ground for Mr Trant who resides within a mile of the place where Mr Ellis was fired at.[12]

The surnames of the alleged 'fellow' and 'ruffian' in the above stories are revealed in an interesting document which will be mentioned in Chapter 6 pertaining to the Ellis murder investigation.

John Ellis is buried in the grounds of the Church of Ireland church in Dovea village. The gravestone is signed: R. Ballantine & Son 18 Up^r Dorset St Dublin.

THE CORMACKS

Though several persons were arrested in connection with the murder of John Ellis, only William and Daniel Cormack were charged.

William was 5' 5" tall, had brown hair, grey eyes and a fresh complexion, while Daniel was slightly taller at 5' 8", had fair hair, grey eyes and a fresh complexion. Their ages on official documents are given as 26 years and 23 years respectively.[13]

Though employees of John Trant, they worked directly under John Ellis. William, who had been with him for thirteen years, was a juryman at the inquest held the day after the murder.[14] Daniel was said to have washed the dead man's body and placed it in the coffin.[15]

They were aware of, and concerned about, a relationship between John Ellis and their sister[16] – which led to 'personal revenge' being nominated as a likely motive for the crime very soon after it was committed.[17] The alleged relationship is a recurring theme in the Cormacks' story.

WHO WERE THE CORMACKS?

There is difficulty in positively identifying the family to which Daniel and William belonged; this is teased out in Appendix I. The Roman Catholic registers for Loughmore-Castleiney show three Cormack couples, with Killahara as their address (as distinct from the adjoining townland Kilkillahara where the murder happened), parenting children between 1814 and 1838. However, the records do not have the combination of all four names identified in the trial as of the same family – Daniel, William, Catherine/Kitty, Anne/Nancy. The most likely parents were James Cormack and Catherine Maher, who married in 1832. James Maher (1826-1914), from the neighbouring townland of Leugh, was known to be a first cousin of the Cormacks. As James's mother was Mary Flood, the Cormack's mother had to be Maher.[18]

The Thurles Poor Law Union rate books for Kilrush ED (electoral division),1844 to 1849, has a James Cormack occupying a house and 18 acres 1 rood 20 perches in Killahara townland. He does not appear in the 1850 rate book where there is an entry for 'the Cormacks and others', and one for a Daniel Cormack. However, these are 'once-off' entries and do not appear in the later books. The explanation for this is that John Trant was liable for rates for his workmen's houses. The rate collector did not enter individual names, but combined all of Trant's liabilities, including land and buildings occupied by himself, in one entry.[19]

There was no James Cormack returned as an occupier in the Primary Valuation list of 1849-50 for the townland of Killahara, but he does appear in the corresponding valuation 'house books'. There is a Daniel, in both the

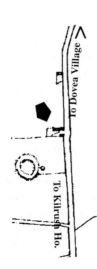

PV list and house books, with a house and 3 acres and 31 perches, valued at £2 17s 0d, and buildings valued at £1 5s. The landlord of the townland was John Trant. The valuation of other Trant-owned houses in the parish ran from four to nine shillings generally, but with a few valued at £1 10s or £1 15s. Tenants in the foregoing types of house had no land attached.[20]

The Cormacks' parents must have been dead when the Ellis murder took place as no reference was made to them in newspaper reports or official documents.

The area pinpointed as their place of residence by a local commentator on the crime in 1857 would appear to be one of the two buildings on the one site in Killahara townland, marked on Ordnance Survey map no. 41, 1840 (left). Their house was not of cabin proportions since it housed William,

Daniel, Catherine, a lodger and his wife and child – which suggests at least three rooms and a kitchen. The house was a place where neighbours met for the popular past-time of card playing.[21] A second sister, Anne/Nancy, was then in Thurles Poor Law Union workhouse where she had given birth to a daughter in September 1857.[22] It was standard practice in those days for unmarried mothers to go to the workhouse for the birth of the child and, perhaps, stay there for some time afterwards.

The names, then, which live on in lore, tragically coupled together, are those of employees of the same landlord – William and Daniel Cormack of the labouring class; Ellis their supervisor and becoming a man of property in his own right.

NOTES

1   Ordnance Survey 1" map no.s 135 & 145, 1905.
2   Devon Commission, Parliamentary Papers, 1844, p. 320 – Ellis's evidence; *NG*, 17 Mar 1858: John Trant said in evidence at the trial that Ellis was with the Trant estate for 25 years; NA, CSORP 1920/8218: Judge Keogh's handwritten summary of the trial, dated 2 May 1858, says Ellis was in Trant employment for 'upwards of 20 years'.
3   General Valuation of Ireland, Co. Tipperary N.R., Barony of Eliogarty, parish of Thurles, p. 92. John Ellis does not appear as the occupier of land in any townland per Tipperary North Family History Research Centre's index of the Griffith/ Primary Valuation for all of Tipperary NR. In the 1901 census the house is the only one designated as '1st class' in Kilrush townland. It had eight rooms. The 1997 facade of the house (photograph p. 7) is substantially the same as it was in 1858. I am grateful to the present owners, George and Bridget Ryan, for permission to photograph their house.
4   NA, Vol. 14/8 LEC; Registry of Deeds, 1852-2-252. Ellis acquired aproximately 22% of the townland of Tinvoher which had 487 acres. The Incumbered Estates Court had been established by law in July 1849. It facilitated the quick sale of land as purchasers were guaranteed clear title. It became the Landed Estates Court in 1858.
5   Thurles Poor Law Union (PLU) rate books, Loughmore E.D, 1855-9, Co. Library, Thurles.
6   Thurles PLU rate books, Kilrush ED, 1850-1, 1855-60 (the books for this electoral district do not survive for 1852-3-4).
7   NA, Vol. 25/33 LEC. Clondoty had eight tenants, only two of whom held their land by lease. Edward Lalor Cambie held approximately 216 acres on a lease that was originally granted 'for three lives' by Henry Robert Carden to a Thomas Bennett in 1820. Cambie had been assigned the Bennett lease with Carden's consent. There is no date given for the transfer from Bennett to Cambie. The

other tenants were: John Carroll, who held 15 acres, also on a lease dated 1820 from H. R. Carden. William Fanning – 57acres; John Gleeson & William Fanning – 46 acres; Patrick Cahill – 9 acres; John Carroll – 15 acres; Denis Gleeson – 4 roods; John Walsh – 1 rood 18 perches.

8   Thurles PLU rate books, Kilrush ED, 1850-1, 1855-60. After Ellis's death the Clondoty farm was held by his representatives. This changed in 1860 and the occupiers were returned as Michael Kennedy: house and 39 acres 1 rood 2 perches, Patt Gleeeson, 12 acres 3 roods 17 perches, Laurence Gleeson, 13 acres 1 rood 16 perches. Michael Moloney is no longer returned as an occupier of a house.

9   Thurles PLU rate books, Kilrush ED, 1850-1, 1855-60. Lahey and Egan continued as Laurence Gleeson's tenants in the houses.

10   NA, Chief Secretary's Office Registry Papers (CSORP hereafter) 1920/8218 No. 07917.

11   *NG*, 26 May 1849.

12   *NG*, 23 Mar 1850.

13   NA, CSORP 1920/8218, abstract from Criminal Register of Nenagh Prison, 1858, made by T. O'Connor, Governor of HM Prison, Clonmel, 20 July 1909.

14   *NG*, 17 Mar 1858.

15   *Dublin Evening Post* (*DEP* hereafter), 17 April 1858, letter signed M.M.

16   *NG*, 17 Mar 1858.

17   NA, CSORP 1920/8218, No. 07917.

18   I am indebted to Michael Maher, Leugh, Thurles, great-grandson of James, for the Maher family information.

19   Thurles PLU rate books, Kilrush ED, 1850-1, 1855-60. Trant paid rates on buildings and 747 acres of land in Kilrush ED.

20   General Valuation of Ireland, Co. Tipperary N.R., barony of Eliogarty, parish of Loughmore West, p. 43-4; NA, House Books, Loughmore West parish. A plaque was erected in 1996 by Leugh branch of Muintir na Tíre to mark the vicinity of the site of the Cormacks' house.

21   *NG*, 17 Mar 1858.

22   Thurles RC parish records. I am indebted to Very Rev. Maurice Dooley, P.P., Loughmore-Castleiney, for informing me of this entry.

Chapter 4
'£100 to any person'

In 1858 the administration of justice was in the hands of resident magistrates, the police and the courts.

Tipperary North Riding had two Resident Magistrates (RM) in charge of districts centred on Thurles and Nenagh, each of whom was 'thereupon to all intents and purposes ... a Justice of the Peace in and for the county'.[1] They were appointed by the Lord Lieutenant whose role was also described as viceroy (king's/queen's deputy) and chief governor of Ireland. In practice the role had diminished to one that was largely formal and ceremonial.

RMs reported directly to the Chief Secretary who was effectively the chief executive of the government in Ireland and was accountable directly to parliament in London. His Irish office was located in Dublin Castle.[2]

The County Inspector of the constabulary reported directly to the Inspector-General of police, also located in Dublin Castle. Co. Tipperary had a County Inspector for each riding, each with a subordinate structure of eight to twelve Sub Inspectors, a slightly greater number of Head Constables, and several hundred constables.[3]

Tipperary North Riding lay within the Leinster legal circuit and came under the jurisdiction of that circuit's Crown Solicitor. The Leinster circuit furnished the judges who presided at twice-yearly courts termed assizes. Offences carrying the death penalty, including murder, were tried at the assizes.[4] Whether the charge proceeded to trial was decided by the grand jury to whom the prosecution presented the case in outline. The constitution of the grand jury and details its functions emerge in Chapter 7. The outcome of the trial was decided by a petty jury of twelve men.

The Lord Lieutenant, Chief Secretary, Attorney-General and Solicitor-General were appointed by the government of the United Kingdom of Great Britain and Ireland and accordingly changed when the government changed. The numerous other offices in the Lord Lieutenant's 'household' and Chief Secretary's office, other than that of Under Secretary, do not impinge on the Cormack story. The Under Secretary was the permanent head of the civil service in Ireland and reported to the Chief Secretary.

From original documents and correspondence, and indexes to correspondence received in the Chief Secretary's office, all of which survive in the National Archives, it is possible to piece together the happenings during the five months which elapsed between the murder of John Ellis and commencement of the trial of William and Daniel Cormack.

The murder was reported by John Gore Jones, RM, Thurles, to Colonel Thomas A. Larcom, R.E., Under Secretary, Dublin Castle, on Friday 23 October 1857, the day after it happened. Having given the late John Ellis the character reference quoted in Chapter 3, Jones concluded his letter by recommending that a large reward be offered and that a detective be sent to the area.[5]

The reply of Saturday 24 October from Henry A. Herbert, Chief Secretary, included an intimation that George Goold, RM, Clonmel, had been instructed to proceed to Thurles to assist Jones in the investigation of 'this outrage'.

Jones's acknowledgment of Herbert's arrangement concluded, 'I have very strong suspicions that private revenge is the motive'.[6]

Herbert's instruction to Goold was by way of a telegram on the same day, 24 October. As it happened Goold was at a court termed quarter sessions in Tipperary town all day Saturday and did not get the telegram until Sunday morning. Understandably, he decided not to go to Thurles until the following morning, and thereby incurred the Chief Secretary's displeasure because 'he had thought fit to postpone until Monday complying with his instruction'.[7] Goold countered this rebuke:

As your communication of 26th instant records the first imputation of remissness in discharge of my duty cast upon me since I became, seventeen years ago, a Public Servant, I beg leave to state the reasons for which I acted in the way that brought that imputation upon me.

Having explained how his absence on duty away from Clonmel prevented him seeing the telegram, he went on to say 'we have never been required, nor expected, to travel or do duty on Sundays except under circumstances of great urgency'. He then dared to say that a competent RM was on the spot in Thurles and that he, Goold, was aware

that up to the late hour on Saturday no arrest had been made, no clue obtained, and I knew by pretty long experience that in cases like the present unless a party is taken on the spot or immediately after the act, several days at least must elapse before the lips of the people who can give information are unsealed. There was therefore no practical good to be obtained in my travelling over to this place on the Sunday, which, from the want of public convenience, would have entailed a greater expense on the public.

On Monday morning I was here [Thurles] at 10 a.m. many hours before even the slightest clue had been reported by the Head Constable who had been deputed by Mr Gore Jones to pursue the enquiries on the spot. ...[8]

Herbert did not accept the explanation, contending that 'it did not alter his opinion as to the course which ought to have been adopted by Mr Goold on receipt of the telegraphic message ...' and that, if the Chief Secretary had not considered the case of 'urgent necessity', instructions would not have been sent by telegraphic message.

This begs the question as to what was so important about this murder as to require Dublin to draft a second Resident Magistrate into the area with such urgency. It may simply be that the importance lay in Ellis's position as agent to a substantial landlord and grand juror.

An official announcement in the *Dublin Gazette* of 3 November followed:

Whereas it has been represented to the Lord Justices that about 12 o'clock on the night of the 22nd October Mr John Ellis was murdered by some person or persons at present unknown at Kilkillahara near his residence in the Barony of Eliogarty in the North Riding of the County of Tipperary. Their Excellencies for the better apprehending and bringing to justice of the perpetrators of this Murder are pleased hereby to offer £100 to any person or persons who shall within six months from the date hereof give such information as shall lead to the ARREST of the person or persons who committed the same.

The above reward will be paid on conviction by John Gore Jones Esq. the RM at Thurles to those who may become entitled to it under the conditions of the proclamation.

A summary of the notice was carried as a news item in the local newspapers.

THE INQUEST

Meanwhile, on Friday 23 October 1857, the day after the murder, Constable Shaw of Killahara barracks, had gathered a jury for the inquest held in the drawing room of Kilrush House, the Ellis home. William Cormack was one of the jurors. RM Jones and Constables Shaw and Douglas were also present. The Coroner for the area was Thomas O'Meara, Bouladuff House, in the parish of Drom-Inch.

The jury's verdict was that John Ellis was murdered by person or persons unknown. This was the inevitable conclusion to be drawn from the evidence of Thomas Burke, driver of the car, and therefore a witness to the murder. One can visualise the anticipation with which the whole attendance awaited his first-hand account of the the terrible event which had undoubtedly shocked the neighbourhood overnight. Burke's graphic testimony was in the form of a deposition:

I am a servant boy of the deceased, Mr John Ellis. On yesterday, about six o'clock, p.m., Mrs Ellis told me to go to meet Mr Ellis to the Templemore station, at 11 o'clock train (the late train). I left Kilrush at 20 minutes past nine, and drove his car through Killahara, through Loughmore, and to the station house. Deceased came on that train from Dublin. He and I drove back by Loughmore (the way I went to the station). When we came as far as Kilkillahara Mr Ellis saw bushes across the road. He asked me to come down and take them away. While taking the first bush a shot was fired from behind the ditch across the car. Mr Ellis fell off the car, and said he was shot dead. I did not see any one. I drove away to the next house and alarmed them; then to the police. It was from Tom Egan's land the shot was fired.[9]

NOTES

1   The Constabulary (Ireland) Act, 1836 (6 Wm. IV, c.13), s. 31 gave the Lord Lieutenant power to appoint resident magistrates at a 'salary by the year, not exceeding the sum of four hundred pounds'.

2   Edward Brynn, *Crown & Castle: British Rule in Ireland 1800-1830*, chapters 2, 'The Executive', & 3, 'The Irish Administration'.

3   The Constabulary (Ireland) Act, 1848 (11 & 12 Vic., c. 72), Schedule A.

4   A government circular instructed that provisions of an English statute, An Act to define the jurisdiction of justices in General and Quarter Sessions (5 & 6 Vic., c. 38), be applied to Ireland. It prescribed that justices of the peace (magistrates) should reserve exclusively for the assizes 'cases which, from the magnitude of the punishment, the peculiar character of the offence, or the difficulties of the investigation, seem more proper for the assizes, such as murder or other capital felony ....' (James O'Connor, *The Irish Justice of the Peace* (Dublin 1915), vol. i, p. 91.

5   NA, CSORP 1920/8218 No.07917.

6   ditto No. 8966.

7   ditto No. 9143.

8   ditto No. 1743.

9   *LR & TV*, 6 April 1858. Burke's statement was printed by the newspaper during the course of its post-trial campaign for mercy, set in juxtaposition with contrasting evidence given by Burke at the trials.

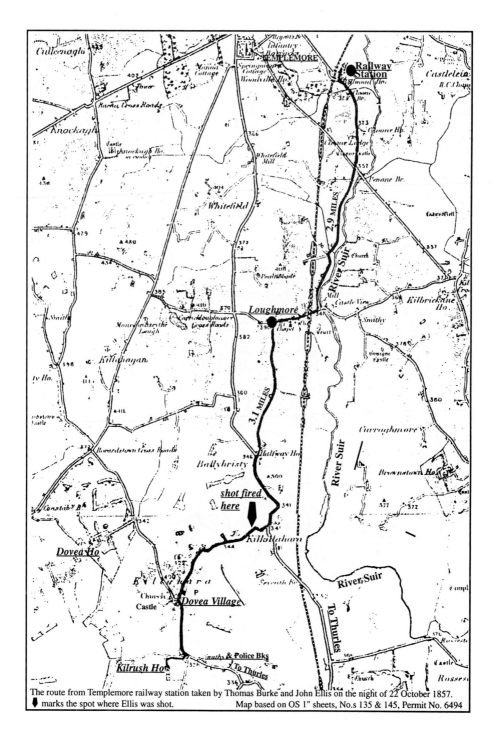

The route from Templemore railway station taken by Thomas Burke and John Ellis on the night of 22 October 1857.
♦ marks the spot where Ellis was shot.

Map based on OS 1" sheets, No.s 135 & 145, Permit No. 6494

17

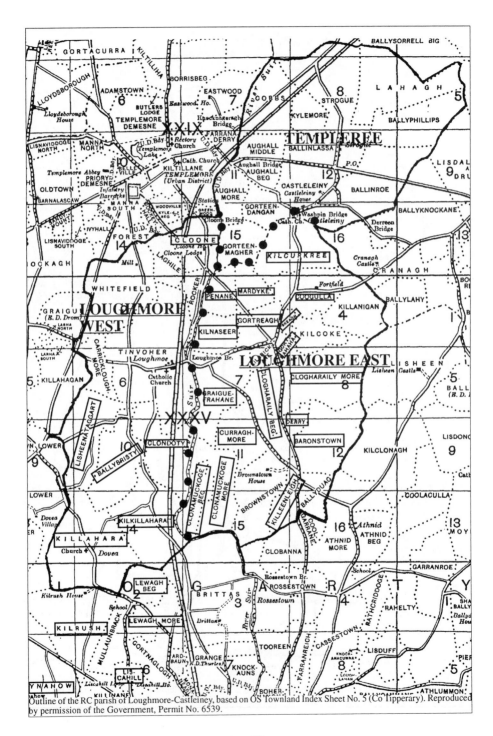

Outline of the RC parish of Loughmore-Castleiney, based on OS Townland Index Sheet No. 5 (Co Tipperary). Reproduced by permission of the Government, Permit No. 6539.

Chapter 5

'The Infliction of the Tax'

Referring to your report of the 23rd Inst. of the murder of Mr Ellis I am directed by the Lord Justices to request that you will state the names of the townlands on which you consider it would be expedient to charge the extra Police Force which will be sent to the district.

Thus Chief Secretary Herbert from Dublin Castle to RM Jones at Thurles on Saturday 24 October 1857.

Jones returned such a list of townlands to the Castle on the following day, Sunday 25 October. It is not clear on which unit (civil parish or electoral district) he based his selection, for most of the listed townlands (shown boxed on the map opposite) were located in Loughmore East civil parish and separated by the River Suir from Kilkillahara in Loughmore West parish where the crime occurred.

Though Jones had supplied the exact – and only – information he had been asked for, Chief Secretary Herbert considered his reply to be 'highly unsatisfactory ... as no reason is given for the selection of the particular townlands, no statement as to the probable participation of the inhabitants in the crime committed, and no information is given to the Chief Secretary to enable him to form an opinion as to the area to which the taxation for extra police should extend'.[1]

The Peace Preservation Act of 1856 was then put into action by a direction from the Lords Justices to the effect

that a force of 20 men be sent ... into the following districts Viz. – the Parish of Loughmore West and the townland of Kilrush in the Parish of Thurles ...

The sum of £175 12*s* 6*d*, being the estimated cost of keeping the force there for three months, was then levied on the ratepayers in the above-named area. Head Constable William Harrison, stationed at Templemore, was nominated 'as a proper person to collect the charges'.[2]

Dublin thus seem to have more or less ignored Jones's list and opted for all of Loughmore West civil parish wherein lay the murder site, plus the townland of Kilrush in Thurles parish where Ellis had lived.

The following interlude in the pursuit of a murder case gives an insight into the several strands of the tax-resistant attitude of the public to the contemporary method of financing the investigation of 'crime and outrage'.

WHAT SAMUEL COOKE BELIEVED

Into the story at this point comes Samuel Cooke (1796-1878), a Roman Catholic gentleman farmer from Brownstown, Loughmore East.[3] Cooke, motivated primarily by concern for the effect that the cost of the extra twenty police would have on his ratepaying neighbours on the other side of the River Suir, wrote a lengthy letter to Chief Secretary Herbert on 13 November 1857, three weeks after the murder.[4] Those parts of his lengthy letter which give information and advice on the conduct of the investigation are set out in Chapter 6.

Cooke's first and second paragraphs outlined the geographical situation of Loughmore East and West, in what electoral divisions their townlands lay, and observed that the land 'was occupied, principally in large divisions and there is little or no intercourse between the people who live East of the Suir with those on the West side, save when they meet at Fair or Market'. He continued by identifying a serious flaw in the application to his neighbouring landowners of the law which imposed on a district the cost of investigating a crime.

4thly, It is submitted most respectfully that the application of the 'Act for the Prevention of Crime and Outrage' to a peaceful district even with the hope of torturing its occupants, by its pressure into giving Information against (most probably) some landless Assassin, against whom the vast bulk (if at all) most certainly can prove nothing, appears to be a plain perversion of the intentions of the Legislature when enacting it – for,

5thly, Such policy (if acted on) would be identical with that so frequently adopted in a hostile country by Commanders who quarter their troops upon the enemy – with this difference: Here they would let Free Quarters on the Friends of Peace and Order.

RM Jones had recommended, and the Chief Secretary had put into effect, two exemptions from this tax for the extra police. They were for the properties of John Trant, Ellis's employer, and that of the late Ellis in Clondoty townland. Cooke's letter tackled the apparent injustice of this and continued with a dash of standard obsequiousness and a hint that Ireland and Loughmore, on the one hand, and England and London on the other, were being treated differently.

6thly, The exemption of Mr Trant's property from the operation of this ruinous statute would cast stigma (strong as Government could fix it) upon all subjected to it; for the obvious inference must be that Mr <u>Trant</u> has <u>not</u> been privy to the murder but that <u>all the others</u> have. ...

8thly, It is hoped that the Right Hon. Secretary for Ireland, whose character stands deservedly high, and from whose liberal administration so much is expected, will not permit his fair name to be tarnished by any measure which must crush the innocent, in his very natural and laudable zeal to punish crime.

9thly, Up to this time there has been no discovery of the actors in the Waterloo Bridge Tragedy, where in a populous city [London] the wretched victim was murdered, salted and parboiled and yet the Government would not oppress the innocent, even in the hope (too oft' a vain one) of extracting evidence against the guilty – They should deem it unconstitutional.

Cooke pointed out that the tax to pay the cost of policing was being levied on all occupiers of land, unlike the rates for poor relief for which the landlord paid all in the case of the very lowly-valued tenancies.

He now unfolded an argument which combined a partial theory on the murder with an understanding, as did his '4thly' point, of the tax-the-locals-into-confession legislation.

... Had the murderer struck down his victim in the daylight – or if the actors formed a party, there might be grounds for harbouring some suspicion that the people know and yet concealed their knowledge of the perpetrators.

But this case is entirely opposite. The murder was committed at midnight.

In a lonely laneway by, I believe, a single person, and without a knowledge of all liable to tax (who, therefore, <u>cannot disclose the name of the Assassin</u> even if Ruin should as is likely <u>to be the consequence)</u>.

Cooke indicated that a formal petition would be forthcoming from the affected ratepayers. This was duly handed in by him within a few days. The concluding paragraph of the petition claimed that his neighbours were quite prepared to pay the smaller tax which would arise if it were shared by all the ratepayers of Tipperary North Riding.

<u>Petitioners have heard that the Magistrates of this North Riding of Tipperary have applied for an increase of the police force</u> which they regard as a wise and salutary precaution and valuing Peace beyond all other earthly blessing, <u>Petrs</u> will cheerfully contribute their proportion of the moiety payable by the Riding for such increase; and detesting murder which too often involves the murder of the soul in the body, they are ready to co-operate with the Government in the exertions to repress it.

The petition was signed by eighty-four people.[5] It elicited the following reply from Under Secretary Larcom.

In the endeavour to reach the criminals and their sympathisers it unfortunately follows that the provisions of the law must necessarily press with severity on many innocent parties, and Their Excellencies deplore such a result but have no power to obviate it. Their Exls have no authority by law to direct the money levied under the warrant to be refunded ... [6]

Cooke now countered that unfortunate-on-the-innocent line.

Under all the circumstances I would respectfully remind you that, as it is universally admitted, it would be better that ninety-nine criminals should escape than that one innocent person should suffer – so, *a fortiori*, it is far better that one or two guilty should get off (even if such should be the necessary consequences) than that hundreds of peaceable, well-disposed persons should be condemned to Exile, or the Poor House.

Some persons of 'l'ancien régime' may fancy that no good can be achieved in Ireland save by the strong hand – that is by oppression – they are wrong. Justice will ever be respected and it commands that criminals be punished but that the Innocent should be protected.

Cooke finished with practical touches calculated to allow authority to climb down without loss of face or force.

If any additional proof were wanting to show the injustice of inflicting such a tax, for such a person, on a people, it is this fact: the mild and pious Rev. Mr Ormsby, the Protestant Rector, had to pay it!!

I am happy to inform you that none of the Tax has yet been paid, and, therefore there is none to be refunded.

In conclusion I beg leave to inform you that, as no Summonses have yet been served, the People still hope that Government will direct the Constable, Mr Harrison, who holds the Warrant, not to proceed further ... .

But a fortnight later, in its issue of 19 December 1857, the *Nenagh Guardian* carried a report to the effect that Head Constable Harrison, Templemore, Government Warrant Officer, 'is serving six days notice afresh on the parties who recently defeated him on a technical point when summoned for the payment of the rate'.

The *Limerick Reporter & Tipperary Vindicator* provided a ready platform, headed OPPRESSION IN TIPPERARY, for 'Your Correspondent, Templemore' with a line of argument remarkably similar to that of Cooke. In its issue of 5 January 1858 the same correspondent continued the campaign.

He argued that the fine or tax of 1s 6 3/4d on every £ valuation of property would amount to only 1s 11/2d if the Great Southern & Western Railway had not been exempted by the warrant from Dublin Castle, and it would amount to only 10d in the £ if in addition Trant and Ellis's representatives had not been exempted. He contrasted the fortunes of 'two respectable gentlemen'. His second instance is obviously that of Trant.

The portion, held by one, is valued at £170. His tax is £13! The lands held by the other (on which the additional police are stationed) are valued at £840. He is exempted from the Tax!! He pays nothing![7]

A trawl through the local newspapers yielded nothing further on the subject and one must presume, in the absence of any reported prosecutions for non-payment of the charge, that Dublin Castle had its way with the Loughmore Westerners.

NOTES

1   NA, CSORP 1920/8218, No. 01966. The townlands proposed by Jones were: Ballyduag, Cloughleigh, Derry, Graiguefrehane, Gortreigh, Barronstown, Gurtnatraha, Clonmackogemore, Kilkcoak, Clougheraillybeg, Killcurkee, Clougheraillymore, Kilnasaer, Clonmackogebeg, Killinleigh, Lisheenataggart, Cloone, Coogulla, Penane, Curraghmore, Skeagh, Mardyke. Loughmore West: Clondoty (Mr Trant's land to be excepted); Killahara (Mr Trant's land to be excepted); Kilkillahara (here Mr Ellis was shot). Parish of Thurles: Leugh, Seskin, Liscahill. Parish of Ballycahill: Ballinahow.

2   NA, CSORP 1920/8218, No. A9378, 6 Nov 1857, signed A. Blane. The Peace Preservation (Ireland) Act, 1856 (19 & 20 Vic., c. 36), was one of a series of emergency measures, in this case commencing on 1 July 1856 and to continue in force until 1 July 1858. It renewed, as did previous statutes, the provisions of the Crime & Outrage (Ireland) Act, 1848 (11 & 12 Vic., c. 2), passed by parliament at the height of the Great Famine, on 20 December 1847 and which was in force for two years. Samuel Cooke used the full title of the 1848 statute in the '4thly' point of his petition.

3   In the 1850 Primary Valuation list for Brownstown in the parish of Loughmore East, Samuel Cooke, a tenant of Captain Goold, farmed 391 acres 1 rood and 37 perches. He also had two tenants on smallholdings and four tenants in houses on a little less or more than an acre – bringing his total acreage to 428 acres 2 roods 35 perches.

4   NA, CSORP Box 771, No. 9759.

5   ditto, No. 10157.

6   ditto, No. 10157, 30 Nov 1857.

7   ditto, No. 9759.

8   *LR & TV*, 18 Dec 1857, 5 Jan 1858.

(above) The bye-road to Dovea village, still only 9 to 11 feet wide, approaching the 'sharp turn with a deep dyke of water'. The dike is still there on the left-hand side between the grass margin and the bank on which Spillane stated he and Daniel Cormack stood to hear Ellis's car coming.

(left) The present gate is where 'there was a way into a field between two posts'. The bank and white-thorn hedge, in which the murderer made a loop-hole, was to the left as one faces the gate.

Chapter 6

'No stranger could have known'

Four days after the murder and three days after the inquest, William and Daniel Cormack were arrested and detained in Thurles bridewell.

Also arrested within a short time were Thomas Burke, Ellis's car driver; Timothy Spillane, an employee of John Trant but under Ellis's direction; John Callaghan, a lodger in the Cormack house; Philip Maher, a local blacksmith; and 12-year-old Anne Brophy, an occasional employee of Ellis.[1] All except Anne Brophy would appear as witnesses in the subsequent trial of the Cormacks. The extraordinary story of Anne Brophy's detention and examination by John Gore Jones, RM, and its sequel of civil court proceedings, is recounted in Chapter 15.

But, firstly, one reverts to the local knowledge garnered by the landowner Samuel Cooke. It was conveyed to Dublin Castle in the course of his plea of 13 November on behalf of his neighbours against authority inflicting the costs of the investigation on them.[2]

3rdly, the road (or rather lane) where the murder was perpetrated, is extremely narrow and impassable. The assassin without being seen, might without help, and in a single minute, have drawn the bushes (which were stopping a gap) right to the spot across the lane; for this lane is lonesome and seldom used, even in the day, [and] must have been quite solitary at midnight, which must have been the hour at which the murder was effected.

Cooke also enclosed a map on which he had marked the scene of the crime and other details. However, after another visit to the murder site he again wrote to the Chief Secretary on 21 November.[3]

On visiting upon last Monday the scene of this murder I found that I was a little inaccurate in marking the spot upon the map which I had the honour of leaving with you on the 13th Inst. I now beg leave to rectify the error, by enclosing a rough tracing from the Ordnance Map of the parish of Loughmore West and the townland of Kilrush in Thurles parish; upon which I have marked several points, which you may wish to know.

A marks the place where the Assassin shot Mr Ellis.

He then refers to the attempts made on Ellis's life in 1849 and 1850 and names the two alleged perpetrators.

The tracing shows the place in Killahara (B) where Mr Ellis was fired at by one Cormac whose father was ejected, who emigrated some time since. The bullet fell from his gun as Cormac leaped out on the road and Ellis escaped with a singed coat. Subsequently he was fired at by one Gleeson (who also left the country) at Gurthnalogh (marked C) and missed.

These two attempts occurred some years ago and had their origin in land.

D is the house of Thos Egan, Snr. It lies east of the high road from Templemore.

E marks the houses of Moriss & Ryan on the same road.

F points out the houses of Thomas Egan Junr, Patk Fogarty.

G is on the road from Dovea to Thurles, is tenanted by several families and is in Killahara. Some members of these families have been arrested.

H the police station and forge in Killahara opposite Kilrush. In this forge pieces of Iron that passed through the body of Mr Ellis were punched.

His summary of the actual murder shows that all the vital facts relating to how the crime was committed were known, notably the position from which the shot was fired, that the murder projectile was not a standard bullet, and the fact that bushes were placed on the road to ensure the car would stop and the driver get down. Cooke now puts forward, in impressive detail, a theory that the murderer had to be a local.

The place of the murder (A) proves in my mind, 1st That the murder had been plan'd for some time previous, by one who knew the locality well. For no one, without thought, could have selected so judiciously, this spot – nor have so chosen it, without being well acquainted with the Lane; for a sharp turn there with a deep dike of water on the S.E. of the road obliged the driver to keep the car close to the side where the Assassin lay. The narrow lane, besides, required few branches to impede the passage: and these were furnished on the spot, where there was a way into a field between two posts fixed in the ground, closed by those white-thorn boughs in lieu of a gate.

The hole broken through the hedge for the gun would also show some forethought – though it would not take five minutes to prepare it. The murderer could not fire until the driver, who was, of course between him and his Victim, had got down to move the bushes. All was premeditated coolly and deliberately executed – and, yet, part of the preparation seems to have been *extempore* [on the spur of the moment], else, the Iron substituted for bullets would not have been used.

2ndly. The murderer must have lived near Mr Ellis. No stranger could have known his movements nor would a stranger venture to expose himself by coming

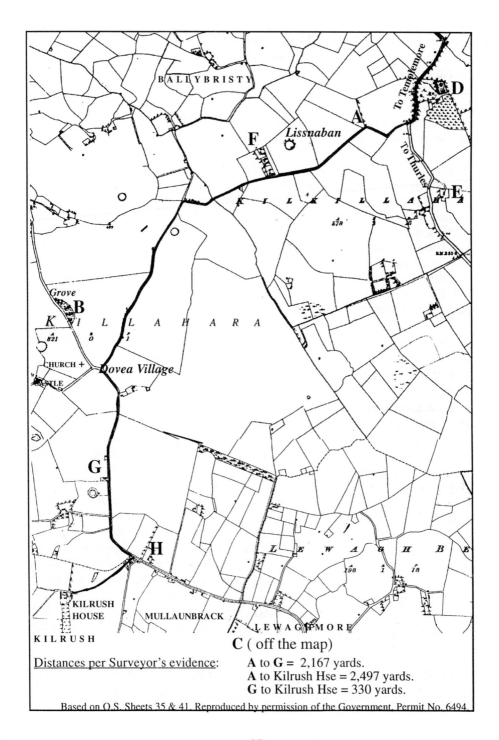

BALLYBRISTY

To Templemore

D

A

F Lissnaban

To Thurles

K I L K I L L A H A A E

578

Grove

B

K I L L A H A R A

821 0 1

CHURCH + Dovea Village

CASTLE

G

H

KILRUSH
HOUSE MULLAUNBRACK

KILRUSH LEWAGHMORE

L E W A G H B E

198 1 18

C (off the map)

Distances per Surveyor's evidence: A to G = 2,167 yards.
A to Kilrush Hse = 2,497 yards.
G to Kilrush Hse = 330 yards.

Based on O.S. Sheets 35 & 41. Reproduced by permission of the Government. Permit No. 6494.

27

any distance – The man who murdered Ellis must have been a neighbour ready to take advantage of the first fitting opportunity for the murder – and must have some grievance real or imaginary to avenge.

Cooke comes very close to 'fingering' *his* suspect who, from later evidence as to where the Cormacks lived, would appear to be either William or Daniel Cormack.

These combined circumstances could apply to one of the persons who have been arrested. He lived near Mr Ellis at the house marked G within 9/10 of an Irish mile (2,030 yards by the line as measured on the map) from the spot where he was murdered. He also lived near the Forge (marked H) where the Iron substitute for bullets was procured. And, if it be true, as reported, that one of the Kilrush police was ill, he must have known it, and that in consequence, the other police would not be likely to patrol that night.

The lands extending far at both sides from the place of the murder, Killahara and Ballabrista, are under grass, lonely and untenanted, and in the occupation of the owner, Mr Trant.

He concludes with some sound, practical advice which coincidentally lent some force to his petition regarding the levy of the cost of investigation on the local ratepayers.

Quartering police upon a people who offer no resistance to the laws, where no illegal association has existence, nor any disturbance of the public, where, in fact, they can have but little to do must bring the force into contempt and excite hatred against them as instruments of oppression. Men's mouths will be cautiously sealed in their presence and even a hint which might lead to desirable information, will not be given.

If a few chosen men were placed at Dovea and Kilrush they would soon become domesticated and would probably obtain more light on this tragical affair. ...

Believe me, Sir, in such a case as this where murder was committed in the dead of night, in a lonely sequestered Lane, though Government may oppress, and even reduce to poverty, numbers of those whom it is its Duty to Protect, it will not, by such means, elicit information. It is not from the tax payers it can be expected, for they cannot give it. A few pounds given to a certain class of persons to drink with fellows, who are in the secret of almost every crime, would probably obtain it. If this means with an ample reward and a pardon for Accomplices doth not gain it, nothing else will.

Cooke includes a revealing description of the murdered Ellis's character in his acknowledgement of Dublin's rejection of the plea on costs. It is in strong contrast with that supplied by RM Jones earlier.

I hope and believe that the unhappy Murderer has few 'sympathisers' in this district – though it is quite true that many, who abhor the crime of murder and would pursue the murderer, if known, had no sympathy for Ellis. His habits were immoral, flagrantly and scandalous immoral. As Steward to a highly respected gentleman, he possessed facilities, and the command of money and used them to effect the ruin of several Females; and it is generally believed that some of their relatives (worked on perhaps by other motives also) avenged their ruin in his blood. Raised from the dregs of his countrymen by his employer, he used the influence he possessed in corrupting Female purity, in immorality in proficiency.

What respectable person could feel sympathy for him.

Had he (a married man) lived under the Jewish Theocracy he would not have been shot – he would have been stoned to death.

THE INVESTIGATION

It appears that in January 1858 the Attorney-General, John David Fitzgerald, MP, authorised a preliminary investigation in Nenagh 'to see how far the case could be corroborated so as to bring it forward effectively at this assizes'.[4] No official report of any such preliminary investigation has surfaced.

There is little enough information in the official records on the actual investigation of the murder and detention of suspects. It is from reports of the trial that we learn when William and Daniel Cormack were first detained. It emerges in later correspondence that they were arrested 'without any private information and purely on suspicion ...'[5] The register for the county gaol, Nenagh, shows that the Cormacks arrived on 14 January 1858, having spent the previous ten to eleven weeks in Thurles bridewell.[6] Thomas Burke and Timothy Spillane were taken to Nenagh on 17 December 1857,[7] but may well have been brought back to Thurles again.

George Goold, RM, writing to Under Secretary Larcom from Thurles in early December 1857 made no mention of the Cormacks by name.[8] From a follow-up letter of 6 January 1858 one learns that Goold had already sent on statements made by Thomas Burke and Timothy Spillane to Larcom.

This is the first official mention of eighteen-year-old Timothy Spillane, son of a policeman, who was to play a key role in the conviction of the Cormacks. Constable John Spillane had been stationed in Borrisokane, where Timothy was born, transferred to Killahara and thence to Co. Kerry two weeks before the Ellis murder.[9] Goold's letter went on:

Our position is ticklish, as, such is the hatred to Ellis's memory that everything will be done to defeat the prosecution and to bring if possible actions against us for detaining these parties. They are aware that a net is closing around them and will [leave] no stone unturned to protect their friends. ...[10]

The dark shadow of an approver now appears, in this case Timothy Spillane. 'Approver' was the legal term for an accomplice in crime who was brought forward by the prosecution to give evidence against the accused in return for his permanent immunity from prosecution. Such a person enjoyed immunity in cases prior to 1861 at which stage the law was changed.[11]

On 1 March 1858 Goold, writing from Nenagh, informed Dublin that his enquiries had revealed that 'a material witness to corroborate the approver is now residing in Cork and that the prisoner's legal adviser has been endeavouring to enlist him against the Crown'. He proposed going to Cork personally to interview this witness. In a follow-up letter of 6 March from Clonmel he reveals that Timothy Spillane, the policeman's son, is the approver:

In pursuance of my intention sanctioned by you ... saw the witness referred to. He is brother to Timothy Spillane the approver, and had been informed that the Prisoners intended to call him to prove that the approver was not out at all that night and therefore must have invented his story.

I examined him at great length assisted by Mr Brew the Sub Inspector ... but whether he had been bought over by the Prisoners, which I can hardly think, or that he feared admitting his brother was out on that night would militate against him, he persisted in stating that he (the approver) was in bed & asleep before 10 p.m. on the night of the murder and never stirred till morning.

This, if true, will shake the whole of the approver's testimony, but we knew, already, that it is false for we have him playing cards a quarter of a mile off till past 11 o'c on that night.

I sent for his brother John, a younger boy, [i.e. a third Spillane brother] who lives at Blarney and had no communication with him.

Being unable to await his arrival on account of our assizes beginning the next morning I requested Mr Brew to have him examined on his coming in. This he did and sent me the result. As he contradicted the first witness materially, I telegraphed for him to Cork by the direction of the Crown Solicitor and he is now in charge of the Police here [Clonmel]. He was examined at length by Mr Dunne, Mr Kemmis's [the Crown Solicitor] assistant and tho' his evidence is not the whole truth, I apprehend, still he discredits his Cork brother. The story of this latter has been told to his brother, the approver, who ascribes it entirely to fear of injuring him. I hope it may be so.

Under that supposition I have communicated with their Father who is stationed as a constable at Ardfert to use his influence to make both tell the whole truth whichever way it turns. I expect his answer the day after tomorrow.[12]

Whatever came of the communication with Constable Spillane is not on record, nor did the discrepancies recorded in Goold's letter emerge in evidence given in the trial.

Meanwhile, on 19 February 1858 Lord Palmerston's Liberal government suffered an unanticipated defeat at the second reading of the 'Conspiracy to Murder Bill' in the House of Commons. Lord Derby (Conservative) succeeded him, Prime Minister now for the second time following a brief spell in 1852. The outcome, as far as the government of Ireland was concerned, was a change of personnel in the chief Irish political offices.[13]

Archibald William Montgomerie, thirteenth earl of Eglinton and fifth earl of Winton, replaced George William Frederick Howard, seventh earl of Carlisle, as Lord Lieutenant. The 'princely, popular' Scotsman from Eglinton Castle had been in the Viceregal Lodge in the Phoenix Park also for the ten months of Derby's 1952 government.[14]

The new Chief Secretary was Richard Southwell Bourke, Lord Naas, MP, eldest son of the fifth Earl of Mayo whom he later succeeded. Naas replaced The Right Hon. Henry A. Herbert, MP, who had been dealing with the Ellis murder case to date. Lord Naas, 'a clever shot', a native of Dublin and reared in Co. Meath, had been Chief Secretary in the 1852 government and was to serve as such again under Derby in 1866 before moving on as Governor-General of India.[15]

Eglinton and Naas, then, came from a society several strata above Dovea House and Kilrush House, not to mention the smaller dwellings of Killahara.

The new Attorney-General was The Right Hon. James Whiteside, QC, MP for Enniskillen, replacing John David Fitzgerald, MP, for Ennis.[16]

There was, of course, no change of occupant of the permanent office of Under Secretary – Thomas Askew Larcom continued his key role in the case.

NOTES

1   *NG*, 17 Mar 1858.
2   NA, CSORP Box 77, No. 9759.
3   ditto, No. 10157.
4   NA, CSORP 1920/8218, No. 13153: letter from Thos Kemmis, Crown Solicitor, Leinster Circuit, 5 April 1858, to the Chief Secretary seeking authorisation to pay G. Goold, RM, £42 2*s* 10*d*, being the expense incurred in the conduct of this investigation.
5   ditto, No. 13646: letter from Kemmis, 23 April 1858, to Under Secretary Larcom to say that none of the reward money was needed for 'private information as none had been received'.

6   NA, CSORP 1920/8218: abstract from Criminal Register of Nenagh Prison, 1858. (the original register for that year has not survived). The register date differs from that on a document signed by Thomas Rock, gaol governor, Nenagh, which gives the commital date as 8 February.

7   *Freeman's Journal* (*FJ* hereafter), 27 October 1858.

8   NLI, Larcom Papers MS 7636, Goold to Larcom, 2 December 1857, seeking permission to return to his Clonmel base to attend to matters left unfinished when he was ordered to Thurles in October. This was agreed to.

9   Borrisokane RC parish records. Timothy Spillane was born in 1840, the eldest of six children born in Borrisokane to John Spillane and Judy Darmody. The couple parented a further three children during the period they were living in the RC parish of Loughmore-Castleiney, the youngest being born in 1857.

10 NLI, Larcom Papers MS 7636, Goold to Larcom, 6 January 1858, mainly concerned with the detention of Patrick Maher, Brittas, who had been named in Timothy Spillane's statement as the owner of the gun used to shoot Ellis.

11 *Kenny's Outlines of Criminal Law,* J.W. Cecil Turner ed. (19th edition, Cambridge 1966) p. 120.

12 NA, CSORP 1920/8218, No. 12343.

13 *LR & TV*, 23 Feb. 1858; Thom's Directory, 1858 & 1859.

14 R. F. Foster, *Modern Ireland 1660-1972* (London 1988), p. 382n.

15 Michael Bentley, *Politics Without Democracy 1815-1914* (London 1984), p. 385.

16 As for note 13.

Chapter 7

The Assizes Commence

The County Gaol, Nenagh, where William and Daniel Cormack were detained from 14 January 1858 to await trial at the spring assizes, was built in 1840-2 following the division of Co. Tipperary into two ridings.[1] The gaol consisted of seven blocks of cells radiating from the octagonal Governor's House. The RC chapel was at first floor level in this building. Prisoners made their way across to the chapel via iron suspension footbridges which linked each cell block to the House. The gaol was designed to accommodate about one hundred male prisoners in single cells. There was a separate set of gaol buildings at the rear for female prisoners.

The extant cell block and Governor's Hse.

The number of prisoners in gaol on 3 May 1858 was 65 males and 18 females. Prisoners were engaged in punitive labour at stone breaking, grinding corn, prison duties and on the tread wheel. Industrial labour for the males extended to shoe-making, tailoring, carpentry, weaving and teasing fibre. Females attended to sewing and laundry. An average of twenty-one persons attended the gaol school daily.

Prisoners were given two meals a day – oatmeal porridge and new milk for breakfast, and bread and new milk for dinner.[2]

The gaol grounds were connected to the basement of the new county courthouse by an underground passage that had been built by prison labour in 1843.[3] Prisoners were escorted along this to the basement. They then went up a short flight of timber steps to the dock of what is now the Circuit Court.

THE SOLEMN ASSIZES

What was called the Queen's Commission, or written authority, initiated assizes – the twice-yearly courts presided over by judges on circuit for which murder charges were reserved. Murder, as distinct from other forms of homicide, had a precise definition originating with seventeenth century jurists: 'the unlawful killing by any person of sound memory and discretion of any person under the King's peace, with malice aforethought, either express or implied by law.'[4]

There was considerable ceremony attached to the opening of the assizes. It must have added to the awe in which the whole business of trials was held. V.T.H. Delany conveys the flavour of such a day in this account[5]:

When the judges arrived in the assize town and went straight to Court, they did so robed, having been met at the railway station, or the outskirts of the town, by the Sheriff with an escort. The judge who was to try crime – 'the Judge in Commission' – wore scarlet robes trimmed with ermine and full-bottomed wig. At the courthouse, the judge was conducted to the Crown Court by the Sheriff.

On entering the Crown Court, the judge in commission stood at his desk, on which his three-cornered hat had been placed. His crier then made two proclamations.... [He called] the name of the judge who was standing above him, and turned and bowed to him. The judge in return raised his three-cornered hat to his head, bowed, and replaced it on his desk.

When the [Queen's] Commission had been read, the judge's crier said, 'God Save the Queen!' and the judge then took his seat. The crier in the Crown Court then said, 'Mr High Sheriff of this County, be pleased to return the several precepts and writs to you directed and delivered or returnable here this day that my Lords the Queen's Justices may proceed thereon.' The Sheriff handed to the judge a roll of papers tied up with tape. The judge received them with a bow, and handed them to the Clerk of the Crown.

There followed the swearing of the Grand Jury. The crier said, 'Gentlemen of the Grand Jury, be pleased to answer your names and save your fines.' ... the Grand Jury retired to their room, and the judge retired to his, where he put off his full-bottomed wig and replaced it with his bob-wig.

The Tipperary North Riding spring assizes commenced on Wednesday 10 March 1858. The presiding judge was William Nicholas Keogh, a Roman Catholic, who was born in Galway in 1817 and pursued political and legal careers. He became a barrister in 1840 and practised on the Connaught circuit. In 1847 he was elected to parliament for Athlone constituency on a Conservative ticket. He co-founded the Catholic Defence Association with John Sadleir and George Henry Moore in 1851. He became a supporter of Tenant Right, joined the Independent Irish party in 1852, and figured in that party's contribution to the defeat of Lord Derby's Conservative government that year. However, to the chagrin of his political colleagues he accepted the office of Irish Solicitor-General from the incoming coalition government under Lord Aberdeen. He was appointed Attorney-General in 1855 and a judge in 1856. He had been the presiding judge at Tipperary North Riding's spring and summer assizes of 1857.[6]

Keogh's preliminary words of his opening address to the grand jury were in contrast to those of the previous year.

I am sorry to find on referring to the calendar before me that it is not now in my power to congratulate you on the tranquil state of your county, as it was my pleasing duty to do on the last occasion I presided in this court. The number of cases for trial, no doubt, is not great, but their character is serious. There are three cases of murder, all of which were attended with circumstances of great atrocity. Four bills of manslaughter will be sent to you and there are two or three cases of old standing, in which bills were found at the last assizes.[7]

THE GRAND JURY

The North Riding's grand jury had an important role to play in the judicial system. These men, appointed at the commencement of the year by the High Sheriff of the county, were substantial landowners and, contrary to folklore, not necessarily all Protestants, as Catholics could be members since the passage of Hobart's Catholic Relief Act in 1793. In practice, however, nearly all were Protestant. To qualify as a grand juror one had to hold land freehold 'of the yearly value of £50 and upwards', or by leasehold 'to the yearly value of £100 over and above the amount of rent payable'.

The High Sheriff was appointed at the commencement of the year by the Lord Lieutenant who made his selection from three names submitted to him by the Circuit Court judges. The High Sheriff was obliged by law to summon the grand jury 'not more than five days and not less than one day before the first day of the Commission/Assizes' and was obliged to summon twenty-three men qualified by law. Each barony within the county had to be represented by at least one member resident within the barony.

The grand jury impanelled for the duration of the assizes had to stay until discharged by the judge. Their duties began after the judge had opened the assizes and they had been sworn in. The oath did not bind them to secrecy. Local government functions of fiscal business – presentments for road and bridge works, malicious injuries claims and so on, for which county cess (nowadays rates) would be levied – had to be done directly after the impannelling.[8]

When that was completed their attention was directed to the criminal business. This extended to studying the bill of indictment, or formal written charge, prepared by the prosecution for each case to be tried by jury, and to endorse it 'a true bill' or ignore it. Endorsement of the indictment meant that at least twelve members of the grand jury believed that there was at first sight a case to be answered. That sent the case forward to be tried by a petty jury of twelve men.

The High Sheriff for County Tipperary in 1858 was The Hon. George S. Gough, Rathronan House, Clonmel. The following grand jury was impanelled at the 1858 spring assizes. The panel had one Roman Catholic member – Solomon L. Cambie. They included the late John Ellis's employer, John Trant. All of them would have experienced a thrill of alarm at the murder five months previously, particularly Bayly who had survived a murder attempt and was himself a land agent as well as landowner.

All were experienced members of grand juries: Lenigan, Phillips, Carden, Sadleir and Bayly had served as far back as the first North Riding assizes, for the Spring of 1839. Undoubtedly, a feeling of clubmanship would have grown up between them and special friendships formed over the years between some members. John Trant's diaries record that he arrived at Sir William Osborne's demesne, Beechwood, at 5.30 p.m. Richard M Carden and James Lenigan were also staying there. Upon returning after the weekend he spent Monday night with Lord Dunalley at Kilboy House.[9]

Sir John C. Carden, Bart., The Priory, Templemore (foreman).
Sir Thomas Bernard Dancer, Bart., Modreeney House, Cloughjordan.
Captain Robert Jocelyn Otway, RN, Castle Otway, Templederry.
John D. Hutchinson, Timoney Park, Roscrea.
James Lenigan, Castlefogarty, Thurles.
Richard E. Phillips, Mount Rivers, Newport.
Sir William Osborne, Bart., Beechwood Park, Nenagh.
John Trant, Dovea, Thurles.
Henry Trench, Cangort Park, Shinrone.
Capt. John Bayly, Debsboro, Ballinaclough, Nenagh.
Thomas Butler Stoney, Portland House, Lorrha.
Richard M. Carden, Fishmoyne, Borrisoleigh.
Capt. Bassett W. Holmes, St. Davids, Urra, Nenagh.
Thomas Sadleir, South Terrace, Borrisokane.
Richard Uniacke Bayly, Ballinaclough, Nenagh.
Lieut-Col. William Knox, Brittas Castle, Thurles.
Major George Jackson, Rapla House, Nenagh.
Caleb Going, Traverston, Dolla, Nenagh.
Samuel M. Going, Liskeveen House, Horse & Jockey, Thurles.
Francis Spaight, Derry Castle, Ballina, Killaloe.
Joshua Minnitt, Annaghbeg, Nenagh.
Solomon Lalor Cambie, Killoran, Thurles.

George Twiss, Birdhill, Newport.

One gets a good idea of the grand jury's legal function from Judge Keogh's address to them at the commencement of the criminal business.

To gentlemen of your long experience it does not require from me any observation on the discharge of your duty; but I may make this remark that unless you are satisfied that the evidence brought before you would be sufficient to justify a petty jury in finding a verdict of guilty, the better way would be, as it would be more conducive to the interest of justice, to ignore rather than find a bill in such cases, because if the evidence is defective and a petty jury pronounces acquittal that prisoner cannot be put on trial for the same offence again, if new, and even convincing evidence should be discovered against him, but the ignoring of a bill by the grand jury is not necessarily attended with the same consequence.

You will pay particular attention to the evidence of accomplices and not find bills on the testimony of such unless it is supported by the corroborating evidence of other witnesses. I have also to remind you that the names of twelve members must be subscribed to each of the bills you may dispose of. You will be so good, gentlemen, as to retire to your room and bills will be sent up to you immediately. Should you apply yourself closely to your business I hope to be able to discharge you before the court rises this evening.[10]

SEVEN KILLINGS

Business in the criminal court commenced on Friday 12 March with five murder charges scheduled for hearing ahead of the Cormacks. A plea of manslaughter was substituted or accepted by the Crown in three cases. A sentence of eighteen months with hard labour was imposed in one case. In another case the sentence was nine months with hard labour, following a recommendation to mercy by the jury 'on account of provocation'. The prisoner was discharged in the third case as he had been in gaol since 3 November and the victim's sister was deemed 'the originator of the whole transaction'. A sentence of 2 years with hard labour was pronounced in the case of a man who pleaded guilty to the murder of his first cousin.

Two other murder cases were heard on the following Monday and Tuesday mornings. In the first case two brothers were found guilty by the jury of manslaughter arising out of election riots, following 'a merciful view of their case' by the Crown. Judge Keogh, however, regarded it as 'a most outrageous outrage, committed in a cowardly manner' and sentenced each to 2 years with hard labour. In Tuesday's case, arising from a fracas which was in the nature of a family feud, the charge seems to have been changed to manslaughter of which two first cousins of the deceased were found guilty. One, who was in poor health as the result of a fracture of the skull received in the row, was fined 6d and discharged; the other was sentenced to 4 months with hard labour.[11]

THE LEGAL PEOPLE

The grand jury endorsed the bill of indictment of William and Daniel Cormack, and accordingly they were put forward for trial on the charge of murder of John Ellis.

The trial, which commenced on Saturday 13 March, attracted widespread attention and was fully reported in the local and national press. James Whiteside, MP, QC, aged 52, who was sworn in as Attorney-General a mere three days previously, was in charge of the prosecution, assisted by John G. George, QC, John Francis Waller, Messrs Henry W. Lover and Henry O'Hara. Thomas Kemmis, Crown Solicitor, was the prosecution's 'agent'. As such it had been his duty to prepare the case for the Crown.

The lead role in assembling the case had been taken by Resident Magistrates Jones and Goold, functioning as justices of the peace. Their powers included the issue of warrants for arrest by the police where required, the conduct of the investigation of both accused and witnesses, the committal for trial of anyone charged with a crime, and the committal to prison of witnesses if necessary.[12]

Charles Rolleston, QC, and Edward Johnstone appeared for William and Daniel Cormack. Their agent was Edward Dwyer, solicitor, Thurles.[13]

James Whiteside (1806-76) had achieved a high profile as the leading defence counsel for Young Irelander William Smith O'Brien in 1848. He was Conservative MP for Enniskillen, 1851-9, and later became MP for Dublin University, 1859-66. He had been Solicitor-General for Ireland in 1852, during the short-lived Lord Derby government when Lords Eglinton and Naas had previously been at the apex of the Irish administration.[14]

John F. Waller had a local connection in that he had grown up within ten miles of Nenagh, at Finnoe House, Borrisokane. He also had first-hand experience of the trauma of murder, as his father, Thomas Waller, died from gunshot wounds inflicted in an attack on him in his house in November 1843. No one was ever brought to trial.[15]

Charles Rolleston (left), aged 52, was a native of Glasshouse, Shinrone, King's Co. (now Co. Offaly).[16] He had a very high reputation as a defence counsel and figured in that capacity at every Nenagh assizes since the first one for the newly-created North Riding was held there in 1839.

Attorney-General Whiteside arrived in Nenagh courthouse at 11 o'clock. Defence counsel Edward Johnstone sought to have the Ellis murder trial postponed until 1 o'clock as Rolleston was engaged in the Record Court. Whiteside would not agree. The matter was settled amicably when it was noted that the time needed for the calling of the panel of jurors and the selection of the petty jury was adequate for Rolleston to complete his other business.

SELECTING A PETTY JURY

Members of a petty jury had to be men aged between twenty-one and sixty. The property qualifications were less stringent than that for the grand jury: they could be freeholders of land to the yearly value of £10, hold land by lease of not less than twenty-one years and of the yearly value of £15, or be a merchant or householder with property of £20 annual value, resident in a town.[17]

These were still men of some substance, even if their league was below that of the gentry of the grand jury. Inevitably, two decades ahead of the modest start to reform of the land laws, a big majority were members of the established Church of Ireland.

The Attorney-General was dissatisfied that only 56 of the 132 people called had made themselves available for petty jury service. It was a typical turn-out: only 37, out of 137 called, were present at the start of the corresponding assizes for the South Riding at Clonmel. A £20 fine (the equivalent of £1,250 in late 1990s money values) was imposed on each of those northerners who did not attend or refused to answer. The panel was called again and four more came on.

It was the potential shortage of jurors that dictated that William Cormack be put on trial on his own, as each prisoner was entitled to peremptorily challenge up to twenty persons on the panel, that is, without any debate.[18] Their counsel refused to agree to a limit of twenty between them. William's counsel then challenged the following persons who accordingly were not placed on the petty jury.[19]

William Ryan, Mount Alt, Ballycahill, Thurles.
Charles Going, Crannagh, Nenagh.
William Waller, Prior Park, Nenagh.
Henry Head, Ryninch, Ballina, Killaloe.
James Birch, Monaincha, Roscrea.
Robert Young, Clonsingle, Newport.
George Birch, Monaincha, Roscrea.
Alexander Carew, Kilbarron, Nenagh.

John de Burgh Dwyer, Ballyquirke Castle, Lorrha.
Henry Franks, Garrytineal, Ballina.
Augustus Robinson, Cloghkeating Castle, Borrisokane.
John Exshaw, Ballyhaden, Borrisokane.
John A. Walker, Ballyduff, Dorrha.
John Hemsworth, Abbeyville, Lorrha.
George B. Long. Ardcroney.
William Minnitt.
John F. Archer.
Richard E. Short, Mill View, Nenagh.

The Crown then directed the following gentlemen to stand down, thus eliminating them also from William Cormack's petty jury. Lanigan, Byrne and Fitzgerald were Roman Catholics.

John Lanigan, Richmond, Templemore.
Dudley Byrne, Ballysorrell, Templemore.
Thomas Harden, Summerhill, Borrisoleigh.
Michael Fitzgerald, Bantis, Cloughjordan.

John Kennedy from Killahara, the same townland as the accused, asked to be excused. The court desired him to remain although he was not eventually called upon to serve on the jury. Richard Biggs also asked to be excused as he lived 'in the neighbourhood of the melancholy occurence' but was refused permission, as was Michael Meagher, Monanore, Toomevara. William Parker, Ballymackey, was excused due to sickness. However, William Jackson was not excused despite a plea that he was suffering from a cold and despite giving evidence to that effect by coughing continuously. Attorney-General Whiteside offered the opinion that coughing 'prevails much among gentlemen who don't like to serve as jurors'.[20] The twelve-man petty jury was then sworn:

George Atkinson, Ashley Park, Nenagh.
Michael Head, Ballinaclough, Nenagh.
William Minnitt.
Richard Biggs, Shannon View, Terryglass.
William Jackson, Cappa, Ballymackey, Nenagh.
Daniel Kennedy, Ballyhane, Templederry.
John D. O'Ryan, Clohonan House, Templederry.
Anthony Nolan, Nenagh.
Hawtry Andrews, Knockanacree, Cloughjordan.

Frederick Evans, Clermont, Nenagh.
Frederick Young, Ballygibbon, Nenagh.
John Phillips, Glenculloo, Killoscully, Newport.[21]

It is not possible to identify which of the two William Minnitts was, firstly, challenged and, secondly, placed on the petty jury. There is a Wm H. Minnitt, Killaun, Dromineer, Nenagh, a poor law guardian in 1858, and a William T Minnitt, Blackfort [Lisduff], Knigh, Nenagh, who died in 1906 aged 81.

Of those twelve, at least three were Roman Catholics – Kennedy, O'Ryan and Nolan.

The prisoner, William Cormack, who is a mild-looking young man of the labouring class, and whose personal appearance and apparel denoted constant employment and comfortable living, was placed at the bar and told he was now about being given in charge to a jury on that charge which, when arraigned on the previous day, he had pleaded 'not guilty'.[22]

The new Courthouse for Tipperary North Riding which opened in 1844. It had a figure of Justice above the pediment. The roof and clock tower of the gaol Governor's House is seen to the right.

NOTES
1   The full story of the division is told in Donal A. Murphy, *The Two Tipperarys* (Nenagh 1994).
2   Appendix to Thirty-eight Report of Inspectors-General of Prisons in Ireland (1859).

3   Appendix to Twenty-second Report of Inspectors-General of Prisons in Ireland (1843).

4   O'Connor, *The Irish Justice*, vol. ii, p. 907, quoting a minor adaptation of the original definition by Lord Edward Coke, 'the greatest common lawyer of all time', in *Institutes* (1628).

5   V.T.H. Delany, *Christopher Palles*, pp. 37-9.

6   *NG*, 13 Mar 1858; F. S. L. Lyons, *Ireland Since the Famine* (London 1971), pp. 106-7; R. F. Foster, *Modern Ireland 1600-1972* (London 1988) pp. 379-84; Denis G. Marnane, 'Land and Violence in 19th Century Tipperary' in *Tipperary Historical Journal 1988*, pp. 76-8. As well as the distrust created by his defection from the Irish Party, Keogh carried a stigma because of his close friendship with John Sadleir, MP for Carlow, a co-founder of the Tipperary Joint Stock Bank, who had also defected from the Independent Irish Party to accept a position from government. Unknown to the bank's shareholders, Sadleir used its finances for speculative railway financing and land purchasing, bankrupting himself and the bank in 1856. He subsequently committed suicide. Tenant Right was a movement claiming an expansion of the 'Ulster Custom' to the rest of the country. This was the right of a tenant to sell his goodwill or interest in the holding.

7   *LR & TV*, 16 Mar 1858.

8   The Grand Jury Act, 1836 (6 & 7 Wm. IV, c. 116), s. 31. Charles H Foot, Barrister-At-Law, *Grand Jury Laws Of Ireland* (Dublin 1861), pp. 1-31. The grand jury's dual purpose structure was dismantled under the Local Government of Ireland Act, 1898, which saw the introduction of elected councils to replace the grand jury in local government – Desmond Roche, *Local Government in Ireland* (Dublin 1982), pp. 30, 45-6. The Courts of Justice Act, 1924, abolished the grand jury in the legal system, and the Criminal Justice (Administration) Act, 1924, provided that all criminal charges prosecuted under indictment should be conducted at the suit of the Attorney General – V.T.H. Delany & Charles Lysaght, *The Administration of Justice in Ireland*, (Dublin 1977), p. 45. The grand jury continued for legal purposes in the United Kingdom until 1933, and is still used in the USA. It originated in Le Grande Inquest as far back as 1166 when Henry II imported the Frankish system from Normandy – Kenny's *Outlines*. For an account of the High Sheriff and Grand Jury in relation to Co. Tipperary, see Donal A. Murphy, *The Two Tipperarys* (Nenagh 1994), throughout.

9   *NG*, 13 Mar 1858; NLI, John F Trant MSS 2566-2573. Trant did not stay for the full William Cormack trial, having left for home at 12.30 p.m. on the Saturday and did not return to Nenagh until Monday.

10   *LR & TV*, 12 Mar 1858.

11   *LR & TV*, 16 Mar 1858.

12   Petty Sessions (Ir) Act, 1851 (14 & 15 Vic., c. 93), ss. 7, 10, 11, 13; commentary by O'Connor, *The Irish Justice*, vol. i, chapter IV, 'Preliminary Investigation of Indictable Offences', pp. 48-97.

13   *NG*, 17 Mar 1858.

14   *Dictionary of National Biography Ireland to 1900*, p. 1399

15 *NG*, 12 Nov 1843. Outside of the courts John Francis Waller was a writer of fiction, verse and lyrics, his best-known song being the 'The Spinning Wheel' (1854), a biographer, editor and rapporteur of law cases.

16 C. H. Rolleston, R.N, *Portrait of an Irishman – a biographical sketch of T. W. Rolleston* (London 1939). Charles Rolleston, Queen's Counsel, added Spunner to his surname in 1867 on inheriting the estate of a Thomas Spunner. He died in 1888 aged 81 years and is buried in a small private graveyard on the former Rolleston estate in Glasshouse townland near Shinrone, Co. Offaly. His children, one of whom was Thomas William (T.W.) (1857-1920), a distinguished figure in the Irish literary movement, did not affix the name Spunner.

17 Jurors (Ir) Act, 1833 (3 & 4 Wm. IV, c. 91).

18 Criminal Law (Ir) Act, 1828 (9 Geo. IV, c. 54), s. 20.

19 *LR & TV*, 16 Mar 1858.

20 ditto.

21 ditto.

22 ditto; *NG*, 17 Mar 1858.

Chapter 8
William Cormack's Trial

The trials of persons indicted on murder charges were conducted in accordance with common law and statutory law. Common law meant the law common to the whole kingdom, defined once as 'a system which consisted in applying to new combinations of circumstances those rules which we derive from legal principles and judicial precedents'. In other words, precedents established in cases decided by judges became the established rules.[1] Statutory law was that enacted by acts of parliament.

Common law, for instance, provided that an accused was entitled to the benefit of any reasonable doubt. Likewise, the evidence of an accomplice, being a person associated with another in a murder, was required to be corroborated. It was the duty of the judge to warn the jury that it was dangerous to convict on such evidence if uncorroborated.[2]

Statutory law, for instance, demanded that the conduct of accomplices should be taken into account.[3] More importantly, it prescribed that the person accused of an indictable offence such as murder was neither 'competent nor compellable to give evidence for or against himself'.[4] In other words, accused persons could not testify in their own defence, nor were they subjected to any type of cross-examination. The only words spoken by the accused throughout the trial were the response to the question, 'guilty or not guilty?', at the commencement of the hearing, and whatever remarks they might make before or after pronouncement of sentence or upon acquittal.

A close reading of newspaper reports of murder trials during the 1830s, 1840s and 1850s shows that the prosecution case generally presented at least two Crown witnesses, of whom one might be an approver, i.e. a self-confessed accomplice – such as Timothy Spillane. The approver's evidence was corroborated by another person who would swear that he or she was in the vicinity of the crime and would identify the accused as the person or persons who fired the shots or struck the blows or whatever.

The defence had to shake this evidence by cross-examination, which was very difficult to do with intimidated and/or well-primed witnesses, and by bringing forward independent witnesses who could give the accused an alibi – the weak link in the Cormacks' case.

The tone and language of the judge's summing-up, together with the prosecution and defence counsels' addresses to the jury, then became vital factors. The jury's verdict, if they reached one, would be 'not guilty', 'guilty', or 'guilty with a recommendation to mercy'.

When trying to piece together a story like that of the Cormacks one has to rely heavily on the local newspapers of the day. Fortunately, their practice of reporting court cases, public meetings and disturbances in great detail, often with additional background material, makes them an invaluable source.

The trial of William Cormack commenced by Attorney-General Whiteside outlining the Crown's case in a lengthy speech addressed to the jury. This, he claimed, was 'strictly according to the evidence to be produced'. He pointed out that the prisoner at the bar and his brother Daniel were in the employment of John Ellis 'or, rather, in that of Mr Trant, and received from him for several years what they had a right to get, namely, a fair day's wages for a fair day's work'.

Ellis was in the habit of going to the Smithfield cattle market in Dublin on a Wednesday and returning on the Thursday. Whiteside gave a detailed account of how the crime was committed by, he claimed, William Cormack and others. He stressed that William knew John Ellis's travel patterns. He then told the jury that the Crown would be producing 'what is called in law "an accomplice"' to the crime.

You will have the evidence of this accomplice and sustained by other evidence which will relieve you from that doubt and difficulty which you would otherwise entertain in a case resting solely on circumstances and the unsupported evidence of an approver. Gentlemen, I have said you will have the evidence of an accomplice. This accomplice was in the employment of Mr Ellis, receiving his pay, and eating his bread. This man's name is Timothy Spillane, and he will prove to you the commission of this dreadful crime by the prisoner at the bar; and during the progress of his evidence he will tell you this: that he saw the prisoner at the bar fire the fatal and murderous shot which deprived his unhappy victim of life.[5]

The *Limerick Reporter & Tipperary Vindicator* newspaper here injected the comment, undoubtedly with accuracy in view of the revelation, 'sensation in court'. The Attorney-General continued:

Gentlemen, you will be told by Counsel for the prisoner that you must be sure the approver is telling you a truthful story – you must be satisfied he was at the place described, and that he was placed in such a position as would enable him to give that evidence which he undertakes to give. Well, I too tell you that you must be satisfied, and, further, I tell you that evidence must be corroborated by some other witness before you can find a verdict, which would result in the deprivation of life of a fellow-creature.

Gentlemen, there were, unhappily, reasons why Mr Ellis might be afraid of losing his life, but it is right also to tell you that these reasons were of a merely personal character, and have nothing whatever to do with ... the setting of land.[6]

At this point the jury were given an extensive résumé of Spillane's deposition (which he himself was to repeat later in evidence). This contained details of when, where, how and by whom, allegedly, the deed was done and named William Cormack as the person who fired the shot. The Attorney-General then gave a summary of the deposition of Thomas Burke, the car driver. This, he held, showed that Burke recognised William Cormack as the person who had discharged the gun at the scene of the murder.

ACCOMPLICE OR CORROBORATOR?

Whiteside now set out with emphasis the reason why Thomas Burke's evidence was corroborative of Timothy Spillane's. He cited

the case of Stubbs, who was convicted on the uncorroborated evidence of three accomplices, and in which case Chief Justice ___ said that the court could not upset the finding of the jury because it was the duty of the judge to tell the jury that they might act upon the unconfirmed evidence of an accomplice. That was a singular case. Three accomplices appeared as witnesses. Their evidence was not supported. There was an appeal on that ground but the court upheld the finding, stating that it was the duty of the jury to act upon the evidence, if they believed it. But he [the AG] was not relying upon such evidence as that, for he had corroboration going to the very identity of the man on trial ...

This Burke is what is called in the language of the country, 'a soft youth', that is, he is not equal in cunning or ability to the prisoner at the bar. He will however prove to you that he heard him [Cormack] threaten his master but unfortunately he did not report that threat ... he says he believed it to be an idle threat and made out of bravado and it would never be carried into execution.

... My learned friend [Rolleston] will tell you, doubtless, that he [Burke] was an accomplice but it will require no ordinary amount of ability to prove such a proposition. He heard his master was to be murdered, but from threats and through fear of consequences he didn't make it known; for he had been threatened that if he divulged a word, or let the ground know what had been said to him, not only would the Cormacks be the death of him, but there would be three others to take their place, if necessary.

At the Coroner's inquest the boy Burke was brought up as a witness and at this inquest there was a circumstance which shows the defective jury laws of this country, for, gentlemen, who do you think was one of the jurors on this occasion? Why, gentlemen, this very man, the prisoner at the bar, who now stands charged with the murder of the unfortunate gentleman into the circumstances with whose death he was sworn to try and enquire – and, gentlemen, it also will be sworn that he contrived to place himself beside the young lad, Thomas Burke, and the latter, overcome by terror, and by a recollection of the threats previously made use of, did not divulge at the inquest what he will prove on the table – namely, that he distinctly saw the two Cormacks and Spillane standing behind the whitethorn bushes, and saw the prisoner fire the fatal shot ... [7]

The prosecution's lengthy address was remarkable in that it attributed no motive for the crime apart from the cursory explanation that it was 'of a merely personal character' and had nothing whatsoever to do with ... 'the setting of land'.

JOHN TRANT'S EVIDENCE

The first witness called by the Crown was John Trant. Trant, a Protestant, farmed 602 acres in the vicinity of his residence, Dovea House. He was also a landlord, with tenants in the parishes of Inch, Loughmore West and Thurles. He had been High Sheriff of the county in 1846. He was a member of the grand jury impannelled for this 1858 spring assizes.[8] However, as can be gleaned from Judge Keogh's address to them, the requirement 'that only the names of twelve members' had to be subscribed to each of the bills they disposed of, allowed Trant, if he so wished, to opt out of sitting in judgement on his employee's bill of indictment.

I live in Dovea; I knew the late Mr Ellis; he was in my employment as steward and manager; he lived in Kilrush; he was twenty-five years in my father's employment and mine; there is a police barrack at Kilrush [actually in Killahara] which is within a mile and a half of my house; ... Kilrush is about four miles from Templemore; there were three roads to it. On the night of the murder I was at Dovea, and was called up and informed Mr Ellis was killed.

I went next morning, about 6 o'clock, to see the place; Burke went to show me the spot; Mr Jones, the magistrate, accompanied me. We examined the place; it was a narrow road turning off the main road; on the left hand side there was a ditch filled with water and a very high bank, and on the other side a bank of earth and heap of stones, with trees growing here and there upon it; the ground was dry and hard, and there were no tracks. From the outside there was a loop-hole but on the inside there was something like an arbour in a garden, with a space opened in it sufficient for a man to stand in.[9]

Trant's description of the arbour and loop-hole suggests that the murderer intended to be fully concealed. This is in some contrast to later evidence of Crown witness Burke that the murderers were visible and recognisable. Under cross-examination by Charles Rolleston, QC, for William Cormack, Trant clarified that 'the hedge on the bank was not a thick one; it was a continuous hedge but not a thick one'.

Trant told how he rode to the scene of the crime while Burke 'went across the fields'. Under cross-examination by the defence, Trant admitted, 'there were some evictions on my lands, but not many; I know nothing of his [Ellis's] affairs except by report'.

Rolleston's question to Trant about the eviction of persons named Cahill was disallowed on the A-G's objection.[10]

OTHER EVIDENCE

Evidence was given by Mrs Ann Ellis, widow of the deceased and mother of their five children, to the effect that she gave Thomas Burke directions about 7 o'clock to collect her husband at Templemore station and that he left ' about a quarter past 9 o'clock'.

> Mr O'Hara – Mrs Ellis, did you ever see your husband alive after that?
> This question seemed to have touched the tenderest chord of affection, and the lady was so overcome by her feelings that she was unable to reply.
> Mr O'Hara said that he would not trouble her anymore.
> Mrs Ellis then left the witness table weeping, and her appearance excited the deepest sympathy of a crowded court.[11]

Sub-Constable William Douglas, stationed in Killahara police barrack, recounted how Thomas Burke, the driver of the car, had called to the barrack at about five minutes to midnight, how he went with Burke to the scene of the murder, examined the dead man and brought the body home to Kilrush House. He explained that the barrack was located almost opposite the entrance to Ellis's home and about a mile from the scene of the murder. He found four pellets in Ellis's clothes in the front of his person – two iron punchings and two leaden pellets.[12]

Dr Bradshaw, who had examined Ellis's body on the Friday,

> found a gunshot wound which entered the back on the left side, taking away the bottom of the blade bone and coming out between the left breast and the collar bone; seven slugs or pellets must have passed through; I could not say what shape the pellets were; the wound was so very large, I made both my hands meet in the body – by putting one hand in the front and the other at the back they met; it fractured the ribs and broke the heart, the person who fired the shot must have been standing very near the deceased, as I think some of the powder entered the wound.[13]

The medical evidence of entry of the shot inevitably means that Ellis, who was sitting on the left side of the car with his own right side nearer the murderer, was in the act of turning, possibly to alight from the car.

THE APPROVER'S EVIDENCE

Timothy Spillane was now called to the witness stand. One report described him as 'a young man with a high conical forehead, small eyes, large cheek bones, and a heavy chin'. This description matches the miniature drawing of a head which Judge Keogh made in the notebook in which he recorded the main evidence.[14]

Spillane gave his age as eighteen years, and said he was in John Trant's employment for about three years and that Mr Ellis paid him. His two brothers were also in Trant's employment under John Ellis. He stated that he knew Daniel and William Cormack for seven years and identified the prisoners in the court. He told of how they had asked him on the day before and on the day of the murder, Thursday 22 October 1857, to go with them to shoot John Ellis and how he had agreed to do so. The newspaper reported: 'sensation at the cool carelessness with which this was delivered'.

He recounted that on 22 October a group, including himself and Daniel Cormack, were playing cards in Cormacks' house at about 7.30 p.m. The group also included Jack Callaghan ('the Connaughtman') who was a lodger at the Cormack's, and two young men, Pat and Andy Cleary. William Cormack was not there as he had 'gone to Templemore for coals' for the Ellis household, but he came in about 8 o'clock and joined the card game.

Spillane recalled that Thomas Burke was also present but left about 8.30. Burke had called in again about 9.30 to light his pipe and told them he was 'going to Templemore for his master'. Spillane said that 'the two Clearys got up, saying their step-father would kill them if they stopped out later', leaving himself, William, Daniel and Kitty Cormack, and Jack Callaghan. Spillane, Callaghan and William continued playing cards until he [Spillane] lost all his money. He continued:

I got up to go away, when Dan gave me a wink to remain outside. The Connaughtman went into his room before I left. Dan followed me out; he said something to me; I understood him; I took off my shoes, and went back into the house. ...

When I went into the kitchen I saw Dan, Billy and Kitty; I then went into the room; Dan came in with me and gave me whiskey; I sat on a bed, and I felt a gun under me. Billy came in afterwards; he didn't drink any, as he had enough in Templemore. Before we left, he [Billy] went out to see if anyone was outside, and John Cormack [no relation] being in the yard, we waited until he went into his

49

house; John Cormack's house was next to Dan's; he then told me to go out.

When I went out, Dan handed the gun through the window to Billy. Dan joined us about 100 yards off. It was then about half-past 10 or nearer to 11 o'clock. We went up along the road till we came to Paddy's Hill, when we turned into the fields, and came out again at Tom Egan's, about a quarter of a mile from where Mr Ellis was shot. When we got out on the road, Dan told Billy to bring a bush, and he said he would not, as we would get one at the place; I then brought it on my back; the bush was to be put on the road the way Burke would get down, and not be shot. We then got other bushes, and Billy put them across the road.

Dan and I got on a ditch, thinking we would hear the car coming. Billy got inside the bush; the road was narrow, and only the cross of a ditch separated him from where Mr Ellis was to pass. I remained there about twenty minutes, when I heard the car coming. I had a stick, it was Billy Cormack's wattle, Dan a bayonet on a rake handle, and William the gun. When we heard the car, we went across the road.[15]

THE FATAL SHOT

Having set the scene, so to speak, for what must have been a hushed courtroom, Spillane now came to the climax of his story.

William was next the road, I behind him, and Dan behind me; when the car came up, Burke got down to take away the bushes, when Bill fired at Mr Ellis; a great flash of fire came out of the gun, and we ran away; we went to a fort, and stood there a minute or two; we came out on the road.

Dan took the gun from Billy, and Billy got the bayonet from Dan. Dan said he'd go to a man named Maher to Brittas with the gun; he did go and we came on; we separated at the house where I slept; I got in through a window. Cormacks lived about a quarter of a mile from that.

I went up next morning to William Cormack's house, and he told me that Richard Coughlan came and wanted him to get up, that Mr Ellis was shot, and he said he didn't believe him. Dan was mending a pair of boots he broke that night; he got them from Mr Ellis.

Mr Ellis often beat me when he caught me idle.

However, under cross-examination by Mr Johnstone, QC, Spillane elaborated on the master-servant relationship. He then switched from the calm demeanour of his earlier evidence to an outburst which caused another 'sensation in court' and must have been a principal factor in Judge Keogh's later assessments of the youth.

Mr Ellis and I never had any dispute, except that he used to beat me in that way. I had no grudge against him. I went out deliberately to murder a man with whom I had no dispute and against whom I had no grudge at all except beating me in that way, or fining me 1*s* or 2*s*. The Cormacks brought me to murder him. I would fire the shot if asked; I would shoot him dead, if asked … I saw Mr Ellis's body after the inquest. I rejoiced when I saw him dead; yes, I gloried in my deed of blood, but I don't glory in it now; I was sorry when put to gaol. It was the love of justice made me give evidence, and not to save my own life.

If Cormack had asked me to murder a man on Christmas Day I would have done it … I would do everything they asked me or would tell me to do … My father used to be following me every day to keep me from them, but I would not stay away.[16]

Spillane said he was arrested on the Friday week after the murder [30 October] and detained in Thurles for three days and then transferred to Nenagh. Six days later he told the story 'of my own free will to Mr Rock [the Governor of the County Gaol in Nenagh] being afraid at the time that my own neck was in jeopardy'.[17]

THE AMMUNITION

Spillane said the gun used was 'long with ridges on the barrel'.[18] On the day of the murder he had stolen some punchings from a forge kept by Phil Maher and given them to Daniel Cormack. 'I put my hand in through a broken window and got them'. He was shown the slugs, and agreed that 'these were the kind I got'.

Maher, the smith, confirmed that Spillane was in the habit of coming to his forge, that he himself punched pellets like the ones shown him in court, and that his bench was below a window. But he could not state whether the punchings found on the body and now produced in court were made by his punch.[19]

Evidence was given later by Head Constable Garrett Barry that the pellets found in Ellis's clothes had a defect that seemed to correspond to those punched by 'a local blacksmith', on whose premises he had found some pellets and a defective punch. Under cross-examination by Rolleston he admitted, 'I won't swear they were made by the same punch. They don't appear so, as one is smaller than the other, and only one has a defect. There was one found in the sweepings and the other at the anvil'.

A cryptic local newspaper encapsulated the confusion among all the participants in court:

The pellets found on the body and those recently punched out of a bar of iron by the puncher with the puncher itself underwent a long and searching examination by the court, by the jury, and by the counsel, but nothing could be made of it, and the result arrived at was that a puncher of same size would punch similar punchings, and that punchings could be picked up in almost every forge.[20]

The card playing in the Cormack house, as recounted by Spillane, and the coming and going of neighbours, reflects a social pattern of the period. It is quite possible that he did steal punchings from the forge. His description of the murder accords with the details of the shooting that were common knowledge – the bushes on the road, the driver getting down and so on.

One notes that Spillane did not implicate himself or the Cormacks for some nine days after his arrest, and that it was not to Thurles-based John Gore Jones or George Goold that he made his statement but to Thomas Rock, Governor of the County Gaol.

Rock, aged 51, was the gaol's second governor, having taken over from the first appointee who was dismissed in 1845 after an official inquiry into the shooting of one prison officer by another. Rock died in 1861.[21]

BURKE THE DRIVER

Thomas Burke, under oath, gave his age as seventeen or eighteen years and said he had been in Ellis's employment for two years as a manservant. He described how he had stopped off at Cormacks' house on his way to Templemore station to meet Ellis. The train was due in at 11 o'clock. 'Dan asked me was I going for him. He did not say who. I said I was'. Burke continued:

I know the prisoner, also Dan, Kitty and Nancy. … There was no one on the car but Mr Ellis and myself. He was on the left-hand side. There is a second turn on the bye-road. There is a dyke on the left hand, and a whitethorn fence on the other. I didn't observe anything on the road until Mr Ellis told me. The horse stopped. Mr Ellis told me about the bushes, and asked what it was about, and when I saw Billy Cormack I got down. He was standing with a gun in his hand behind the ditch. I saw Tim Spillane and Dan behind him. William had the barrel of the gun through the bush. I saw his face distinctly. It was a bright night. After I jumped off the car a shot was fired from the right-hand side, where I saw the gun. Mr Ellis fell immediately. The car wasn't a yard from the gun. When I saw him fall I went and asked him was he shot, and he made no reply.

I then drove to Ned Coghlan's. There were two boys living there, workmen of Mr Trant. I then went to call Joe Davis. I saw George Coghlan at his house. I did not see Joe Davis, but he answered me. I then went up to the police barrack. I returned with them to where Mr Ellis was killed, and found him lying on the broad of his back across the road. His body was not in the same position as when I left. He was then lying by the dyke. …

I saw the jury sitting on the inquest. William Cormack was there. He was standing by my side. He said nothing to me then. I saw him after in the stable and he said I did well not to answer the skulkers from Thurles as they were worse than Mr Fox or Mr Goold. The skulkers were Mr Johnstone and Patt Davy. They were on the inquest. Davy asked me questions … [22]

In reply to questions put by Counsellor Rolleston, Burke said:

> When I saw William with the gun in his hand, just previous to its being fired off, half his person was exposed above the hedge.
>
> ... I was asked [at the inquest] did I go into Cormacks, and I said I did not. ... did I see anyone inside the ditch, I said not. I could not tell the truth, because Billy Cormack was there.
>
> I had no suspicion Mr Ellis would be shot. Dan met me on the road the day of the murder. He told me he was putting me on my guard, and he didn't like to have the death of me. I asked him what spite he owed to me, and he said he did not, but Ellis.
>
> He [Dan] said that he might not shoot me, he'd put a stoppage on the road, and now I put you on your guard, and if you let the ground know it I'll get three men, that know it as well as I do, to shoot you. When I saw the stoppage I knew what it was about, and I got down to save my life.

When exactly Burke had met Daniel Cormack was clarified in his re-examination by the prosecution's Mr George. 'It was at the time I was walking up to Dan Cormack's that he spoke to me about the murder'. This was earlier on the night of 22 October and might even have been before Mrs Ellis instructed him to proceed to Templemore to meet the train.

In further evidence Burke stated that a long time previous to the murder he had given lead from Ellis's store to Timothy Spillane and, a month before the murder, blasting powder to William Cormack that he had purchased in Thurles for Mr Ellis.'

Under further cross-examination by Rolleston, Burke clarified that he 'was taken the Tuesday morning after the murder' and detained in Thurles for five weeks before being transferred to Nenagh. 'It was I first told about him' [Spillane]. He said he was examined several times by Mr Goold and Mr Jones but that it was to Mr Rock that he 'told for the first time all I knew.' He stated that Mr Jones had told him, 'you may stop in gaol till you rot'.[23]

Burke's statement that it was he told, presumably Jones and Goold, about Spillane is tantalising as the context is not known. Burke clearly implicates himself in the incident by admitting that he knew in the event of an ambush on Ellis that bushes would be put on the road to bring the car to a halt. He held off identifying William Cormack as the murderer for nearly six weeks.

Burke's evidence that he recognised three people at the scene is not entirely credible. It seems highly unlikely that the murderer, knowing that Ellis would be accompanied, would have left himself visible. Trant's description of the arbour suggests that he did not.

One hears for the first time of RM Jones's alleged threat to him. However the defence did not make any effort to establish if it had been uttered. Neither did they draw an analogy between the effect a threat like that might have on him and the effect which Burke claimed William Cormack's presence had on him at the inquest. The words of this alleged threat were to become a virtual refrain throughout the case and its aftermath.

Thomas Rock's part in obtaining his confession cannot be verified.

No one took up Burke's statement, then or later, that Ellis's body had changed position on the road. It may be that Ellis was still alive when Burke fled, and that he managed to move slightly before he expired.

MORE WITNESSES
Other witnesses called by the prosecution included Jack Callaghan, the Cormacks' lodger. He described how, after Burke and the Cleary brothers went away, the other card players continued until

> I went into my bedroom and said my prayers, having a penance to perform. I then got a rush, and divided it in two, and I brought out one half to William Cormack, as his candle was burned out. He said to give it to Dan. I went in, and after a few minutes I saw the light quenched. The door then opened and I heard feet going to the door. It was about ten to eleven o'clock. I never knew a word of the murder until the morning after.[24]

Callaghan told the court that he was arrested fifteen days [on 6 November] after the murder and detained for ten days in Thurles bridewell. William and Daniel Cormack were also held there. He spoke to Dan but could not recollect the content of their conversation.

John Sadleir, Superintendent of Thurles bridewell, said in evidence that he had eavesdropped on a conversation between Callaghan and Daniel Cormack during their detention in Thurles, and on Daniel's relay of that conversation to William to allay William's fear that Callaghan might have said anything about their going out on the night of the murder. Sadleir added that William said 'tell him not for his life to say we went out that night or that I was drunk'. What excited his suspicion and induced him to watch the prisoners was a systematic coughing they had amongst them.

In a subtle way these two witnesses appeared to confirm the Cormacks' alleged implication in the murder. Firstly, Callaghan by suggesting that the Cormacks were out of their house around the time the murder was committed and, secondly, Sadleir by conveying the impression that they had reason to

54

be anxious about what Callaghan had said under examination.

THE DEFENCE COUNSEL'S AND JUDGE'S ADDRESSES

The only witness for the defence called was Catherine (Kitty) Cormack, who stated that her brothers did not go out on the night in question. She admitted, in the course of a cross-examination at great length by the Attorney-General, that she heard Richard Coghlan call her brother in the early hours of the following morning but that he did not get up.

Mr Rolleston in his address to the jury emphasised that there was no evidence given that could convict, only that of Burke ('an accomplice both before and after the murder') and Spillane. He drew the jury's attention to the unreliable nature of Burke who 'knew of his master's danger and yet led him to the slaughter, and who at the inquest denied all knowledge of the man who fired the fatal shot'.[25]

Judge Keogh addressed the jury for two hours, most of which went on a full recapitulation of the evidence.

... though a jury should secure the testimony of approvers, judges always advised that their evidence should not be acted on unless corroborated; that here Spillane, that most atrocious savage, who was ready for every deed of blood, was the principal witness and that, unless he were corroborated, no man would be safe were his evidence alone to be considered sufficient.

But it was for the jury to say whether the other facts would warrant them in arriving at the solemn conclusion which would deprive a fellow man of his life, and send him to an ignominious grave. They had the evidence of Burke, who, though not an accomplice, had acted in a manner most discreditable. But there were untainted witnesses in the case, and the jury would decide whether their testimony sufficiently corroborated the statements of Spillane and Burke.[26]

JURY OUT

This concluded the lengthy hearing, during which the jury had heard very damning evidence from an approver and corroborating witness – given, it must be said, convincingly. But doubts as to its veracity rest on the fact that both only admitted their involvement after a fairly lengthy detention and, obviously, after interrogation by Governor Rock. RM Jones's alleged remark to Burke, 'you may stop in gaol till you rot', was threatening and intimidatory. However, as John Gore Jones was not a witness, he could not be challenged as to whether that accusation was accurate.

The jury retired at 9 p.m. At 11 p.m. the foreman, when called to the box, stated that no verdict had been reached. One juror requested that a portion of the evidence be read over to him, and this was done. The newspaper report does not say which portion. It does, however, comment that the judge 'declined to offer an opinion as to the character of the evidence', and said 'it was the province of the jury to attach such weight to the evidence as they considered it deserved'. At midnight the jury again retired and were locked up under guard for the night.

At this point the Crown's legal representatives emphasised to the judge the need to have a full attendance of jurors present on Monday, as, 'whatever the verdict of the jury now might be', they intended to press on with the trial on Monday (apparently, meaning Daniel's trial, as the verdict had not been brought in on William's). The onus was then placed on the sub-Sheriff, Gerald Fitzgerald, to ensure a full attendance of jurors, a task possibly made easier by the fact that Judge Keogh indicated that he would fine absentees heavily. Mr Fitzgerald told the court that some of the jurors called had told his bailiff they would not attend. It was arranged that special messengers be sent to jurors on the list to request them to be present on Monday morning.

At 9 o'clock on Sunday morning news was conveyed to the judge that one of the jurors on the night-long sitting had been taken ill. On investigation it transpired he was 'only very weak from want of sleep and food'. All twelve were then recalled to the court. After clarification of some points of Burke's evidence they retired again.

They were then twelve hours in confinement without reaching a verdict. They were again recalled at 4.30 p.m. on the Sunday and, Daniel Kennedy's illness having been confirmed by the gaol physician Dr O'Neill Quin, they were discharged.[27]

They had failed to reach a verdict after a total of nineteen and a half hours deliberation.

NOTES

1   *Encyclopedia Britannica*, vol. 6, p. 122, authorship unattributed but referencing such famous jurist-writers as Blackstone, Holmes, Pollock, Dicey.

2   William Feilden Craies and Sydney L Phipson in *Encyclopedia Britannica*, vol. 23, p. 690a; Anon, vol. 1, p. 101c; Kenny's, *Outlines*, p. 522.

3   Kenny's, *Outlines*, p. 484.

4   Evidence Act, 1851 (14 & 15 Vic., c. 99), s. 3.

5   *LR & TV*, 16 Mar 1858.

6   ditto.

7   *NG*, 13 & 17 Mar 1858; *LR & TV*, 16 Mar 1858. The *LR & TV* carried verbatim reports of the addresses and evidence whilst the *NG* leaned towards summaries.

8   General Valuation of Ireland, Co. Tipperary, barony of Eliogarty, 1849-50, p. 29. John Trant's diaries, extant in NLI for the years 1851-8, show that he was involved in the arrangement of Ellis's funeral and assisting Mrs Ellis in sorting out legal and monetary business. He came into conflict with his tenants and the local Land

League in the early 1880s and was boycotted. For his personal memoir of that event see Elaine Burke Houlihan, *Tipperary: A Treasure Chest* (Nenagh 1995), pp. 43-50. John Trant died in 1887, aged 68 years, and is buried in the same graveyard as John Ellis, beside Killahara church in Dovea village

9   *LR & TV*, 16 Mar 1858. The field from which the fatal shot was fired is on the land of Paddy and Frances Egan and still has the same bounds apart from the roadside ditch.

10   ditto.

11   *NG*, 17 Mar 1858.

12   *NG*, 17 Mar 1858; *LR & TV*, 16 Mar 1858.

13   *LR & TV*, 16 Mar 1858.

14   Keogh MS Noteboook, p. 107. A copy of the notebook was kindly loaned to me by Very Rev. Maurice Dooley, P.P., Loughmore-Castleiney. The original is in St. Patrick's College, Thurles.

15   *NG*, 17 Mar 1858; *LR & TV*, 16 Mar 1858.

16   ditto.

17   *LR & TV*, 16 Mar 1858.

18   According to Judge Keogh's MS notebook, p. 108, Spillane told a juror it was a 'long gun with ridges up the barrel, no sights on it. There was a piece out of the mouth'.

19   *LR & TV*, 16 Mar 1858.

20   ditto; *NG*, 17 Mar 1858.

21   Appendix to Twenty-Sixth Report of Inspectors-General of Prisons in Ireland (1847).

22   *NG*, 17 Mar 1858.

23   ditto & *LR & TV*, 16 Mar 1858.

24   *NG*, 17 Mar 1858.

25   ditto.

26   ditto.

27   ditto; *LR & TV*, 16 Mar 1858.

Chapter 9
A Joint Trial

The court resumed at 9.30 a.m. on Monday 15 March. After disposing of another murder case as recounted in Chapter 7, William and Daniel Cormack were now placed on trial together, indicted for the wilful murder of John Ellis. 83 jurors were available, plus the 12 in the Record court which was dealing with civil/non-criminal cases under a second judge. The judge imposed a fine of £50 each on non-attenders, the equivalent of over £3,000 in late 1990s values.

Counsel for both sides agreed that the prisoners be jointly allowed to challenge up to thirty jurors and that the twelve who had served on William's trial be exempted. Those challenged and set aside included the following who had also been challenged for William's trial on the Saturday:

William Waller, Henry Head, James Birch, Robert J. Young, John de Burgh Dwyer, Henry Franks, Augustus Robinson, John Exshaw, John A. Walker, William Minnitt.

The following were also challenged and not placed on the new petty jury:

Nicholas Biddulph, Congor House, Ardcroney.
James J. Poe, Solsboro, Nenagh.
Peter Smithwick, Shanbally, Nenagh.
Edward Sanders, Greyfort, Borrisokane.
Robert Lowe, Templetuohy.
Percy J. Poe, Brooklands, Co. Limerick & Nenagh.
William Abernethy, Oak Park, Carrig, Birr.
Toler Woulfe, Ballyanny, Nenagh.
Montague St Leger, Bessboro, Ballymackey, Nenagh.
Robert Neville, Townparks, Roscrea.
Henry Hunt, probably Templederry.
John B. Long, possibly Ardcroney
Vizier Bridge, Ashbury, Roscrea
George F. Amber.
Timothy Bridge, Millpark, Roscrea

Edmond Parker.
Edmund Maunsell, possibly Newport.
Robert T. Nye.
John Parker, Ballycolliton or Brookfield, Nenagh.

The Crown again ordered Thomas Harden, Summerhill, Borrisoleigh, and Michael Fitzgerald, Bantis, Cloughjordan, to stand down, and added the following:

Samuel Cooke, Brownstown, Loughmore.
William Kennedy, Coolamunna, Cloughjordan.
Michael Meagher, Monanore, Toomevara.
Samuel Dudley, Tinderry, Knock, Roscrea.
David Brindley, Castle Street, Nenagh.

At least four of those were Roman Catholics – Cooke, Fitzgerald, Kennedy, and Meagher. However, there were three Roman Catholics, Smith, Roche and James Mason, among the twelve petty jurors then sworn to try the case:

Horatio Lloyd, Mount Frisco, Dunkerrin.
Solomon Baldwin Cambie, Kilgarvan, Nenagh.
Peter Bayly, Shannonvale, Nenagh.
John J. Smith, Milford, Borrisokane.
Henry Phillips, Bushfield, Nenagh.
Richard Mason, Adamstown, Templemore.
John J. Short, Pallas, Lorrha.
Thomas Grey, Ballingarry, Roscrea.
Nicholas Roche, Ballinamona, Nenagh.
William Exshaw, Aglishcloghane.
G.W. Bassett, Newport Mills.
James Mason, Bellwood, Templemore.

EXTRA EVIDENCE

Witnesses called at William Cormack's trial on Saturday were then re-examined. John Trant added to Saturday's evidence an opinion which was helpful to the prosecution: 'If the prisoner was standing in the arbour, he could be seen from his waist up'. 'Under cross-examination by the defence he said that three men could be seen from the road 'as the ground rises from the ditch'. He confirmed to the court that 'a person on a car, coming opposite the place, could see the three men. The road is level'. This evidence certainly abated the impression given by his Saturday evidence that the murderer may have been concealed by the hedge.

Trant further stated that Ellis's life was in danger up to three or four years ago but that it ceased then.

Approver Timothy Spillane, under cross-examination, said that about a fortnight before the murder, Daniel Cormack told him that he and William were going to kill Ellis 'on account of his sister'. Later, in response to a question put by juror Lloyd, he said, 'Kitty, who gave me the whiskey, was the woman who was spoken about'.

He also said that he had seen the gun used to murder Ellis in Daniel Cormack's possession about three weeks beforehand when Cormack 'went out to shoot a man named Roche, Mr Trant's herd. Pat Maher of Brittas owned the gun'.

We now know that Nancy Cormack had had a child for a man named Roche seven weeks before the murder.[1]

Spillane's cross-examination by Counsellor Johnstone for the defence yielded the following demonstration of what could be understated as a lack of balance in the witness:

I am a Catholic. I go to Mass sometimes – about six times every year. I prayed for myself and no one else. I prayed to God to give me more grace to pass my enemies. I would not commit the murder myself. I never would think of the like. I didn't put my hand on Mr Ellis at the inquest, as I was afraid he would throw up blood and I'd be taken on the spot. I often heard that when a man was murdered he would throw up blood if the person went near him. If Mr Ellis was not shot that night, I might go again if asked. I wouldn't go myself.

I don't want to hang them, let ye get someone else (laughter). I don't know about a reward being offered. I never read a notice on a police barrack. I don't want money. If it was given me, sure I would not throw it away. If I was offered money by the Crown, I would not take it. If I was asked by my friends, I would not commit another murder. (The witness here commenced to cry.)

Burke gave some additional evidence to that given in Saturday's trial. He introduced an account of a meeting he claimed to have had with Daniel Cormack about five weeks before the murder. The sister referred to in this account has to be Catherine/Kitty as Nancy was in Thurles workhouse at the time of the incident described by Burke.

I was in a shed of Mr Ellis's, where they were making ropes. Mr Ellis came out, and when I saw him I hid, because it was not my place. When Mr Ellis went away, Dan said he'd be the death of him. I didn't say anything. About a fortnight before the murder Dan came to the coach house where I was, and asked me did I see Mr Ellis and his sister together. I said not. He said if he found it out he'd be the death of him. ... if he had thought that Mr Ellis had made a bad character of his sister, he would have his life. I never told anyone of the threats.

It was through the bushes I saw his head and body. I hadn't got as far as the horse's head, when the shot was fired.[2]

Richard Coghlan said that when he went down to Cormacks' house to call them up there was a light in Callaghan's room window – it might have been firelight. He lifted the latch of the door but it was fastened. He went to Cormack's window and said 'Billy, Billy, get up, Mr Ellis is killed,' and he replied, 'go to the Devil, is he shot?' I asked was Dan there, and he said he was, but Dan never spoke'.

It is puzzling that Billy or Dan did not get up when they heard that Ellis was killed. This was held against them by Keogh in his summing up.[3]

Head Constable Barry was examined by prosecuting counsel Lover, and said he considered the small-sized pellets had been made by the punch owned by Phil Maher.

Andrew Cormack, a neighbour of the Cormacks but not related to them, gave evidence to the effect that he had called to their house on the morning after the murder. Spillane, who was a lodger in his house, was also there. In a discussion on the Ellis murder a Dan Maher accused Spillane of doing the shooting, to which William Cormack replied, 'whoever shot Mr Ellis had more courage than Tim.'

John Callaghan recalled the conversation he had with Daniel Cormack in Thurles bridewell:

Dan said to me, 'were you tried?' and I said 'yes'; he then asked me did they search the house, and I replied I thought they did; and did they get anything, he enquired, I said nothing but a blackthorn stick ... Another day after this Dan was speaking to me, and he said, we will soon be expecting a trial, and you can tell Mr Jones the door was shut when you went to bed, and that it wasn't opened afterwards, or couldn't be opened unknown to you. We often had conversations after but I forget what they were.

Defence counsel Rolleston pursued the question of the comings and goings at Cormack's house in the night. Callaghan said,

... I heard the noise crying through the kitchen, and then I heard the door open, the same as if persons were going in and out; I heard no more that night. ... I might tell a lie but I would not swear one, for a thousand pounds.

John Sadleir, the Thurles bridewell keeper, was also recalled to give his account of the Cormack-Callaghan conversation on which he had eavesdropped.

Burke was also in the Bridewell. I was in the yard one day, and I heard Dan tell Burke to hold his holt; I went over to Cormack and asked him why he spoke to Burke; he denied it first, but acknowledged it afterwards.

Under cross-examination by Counsellor Johnstone, Sadleir revealed that he had reported that conversation the following day to RM Jones. At this point he also recounted conversations between the two Cormacks who were 'only about 7 feet asunder' at their cell windows.

I heard William caution Dan not to say anything. I cautioned them several times about their speaking, and told them they would rue it. I heard three conversations before I gave the warning. At the time I heard the conversations I did not know I would be examined.

It emerged later that the prisoners had not been informed of Sadleir's allegations in advance of the trial. Hence their counsel had no chance to prepare a line of questioning which might discredit him.

The only alibi for the brothers came from their sister Catherine and Mrs Mary Callaghan the lodger who stated under oath that the Cormack boys did not go out of the house the night the murder was committed. There is no mention in the newspaper reports of Mrs Callaghan having given any evidence at William Cormack's trial two days previously.

THE DEFENCE

The cumulative newspaper accounts of this second trial, particularly in relation to Counsellor Rolleston's closing speech to the jury, are more comprehensive than for William's trial. According to the *Nenagh Guardian* report, Rolleston

addressed the jury in a powerful speech on the part of the prisoners, contending, as he did in the former case, that Burke was an accomplice both before and after the fact – that he knew his master was to be murdered on the very night when the murder really did take place, that he drove the victim into the very teeth of the murderers, and that after the act was committed he held his peace, although he now swears against the prisoners at the bar, charging them by his evidence with the commission of that barbarous offence, his only ground for excuse for not denouncing them at once being that in the first instance he did not think the offence would be committed, and that the threat of murder was only an idle one, and never would be put into execution, although he told the murderers – supposing the prisoners at the bar to be the guilty parties – the hour at which his master would return; and in the second instance, and after the deed was committed he remained silent, pleading fear for not denouncing them at once, although he was in the presence of the coroner, surrounded by the spectators, and standing under the protection of the police.[4]

Give me evidence, said Mr Gore Jones, the stipendiary, to the car-driver Burke, Spillane's associate – 'give me evidence, else, if you do not, I'll keep you in gaol till you rot' … and, as the witness added when cross-examined, 'after you rot'.

Rolleston had at that point, as far he was concerned, demolished the character of the approver's corroborating witness, Thomas Burke. He now turned to the prosecution's prohibition on exploring an alternative motive to one of 'personal revenge' for Ellis's murder. He went on to outline his perception of the unlikelihood of the Cormacks, even if they had a motive, engaging Spillane as an accomplice.

• I wanted to ascertain a motive on the part of the accused for the commission of this most foul crime; but I was stopped in the course which I was pursuing to attain that object by the Attorney-General, who prevented me from asking Mr Trant were there not evictions on his property during the agency of Mr Ellis? I cannot tell what might have been the result of my enquiries upon this point, it might have been, perhaps, to show you that the prisoner at the bar was not evicted, that he had no land from which to be turned adrift, and that, so far, he could have no motive, personally, which would induce him to commit murder on the man who was giving him bread to earn; but you are aware, gentlemen, that I am standing in a county that was once infamous for the commmission of agrarian outrages … and am I to be told in this same county, where persons who stood in the high position of the Attorney-General have established the eviction from land as a motive for murder – am I to be told, I repeat, in this county that eviction here was not the probable motive for murder. Were there any persons evicted? Was there no ill-feeling excited by legal proceedings touching land? Was there no bad feeling existing between the evicted and the deceased which may have been looked upon as the instrument of their eviction?

• Do you not think, gentlemen, that if the Cormacks had an intention to murder Mr Ellis that their acting in this way did not display that species of intelligence which marks our peasantry beyond those of any other country on earth? Would any one of them ask a man to commit a crime he having no weapon suited for the commission of the offence … or do you think that they would have entrusted their intention to murder a man, against whom they had no malice whatever, to the keeping of a third party? ... They would have committed the murder themselves, and not jeopardised their lives by placing them in the hands of the son of a policeman, who, at any moment, and with a reward staring him in the face, aye, could, and would, deliver them up to the outraged laws of their country.

The counsel's wide-ranging address to the jury, which ran to over four columns of the *Limerick Reporter & Tipperary Vindicator* when quoted verbatim, now attacked the inferences drawn by the Attorney-General in relation to the punchings fired from the gun, allegedly stolen by Spillane from the forge on the Cormacks' behalf; then in relation to the comings and goings from the house on the night of the murder; and finally in relation to the Cormacks reaction and non-reaction to the news of the murder brought by a neighbour.

•   There is no more public place in the community than a blacksmith's forge, men go there to smoke – to argue politics – to discuss the news – to chat about the weather – to inquire about the markets, and sometimes to hear and to circulate some scraps of village scandal, and there is not a man in the world who has a four-footed beast but might go in there and poke up these punchings if he required them. ... the blacksmith has demonstrated to you that the punchings found on the body of Mr Ellis could not have been punched with his punch, which was too large. ...

•   Spillane has sworn, that in consequence of a wink from Daniel Cormack, he went out, and remained outside until brought back again by Daniel Cormack – Now, the Connaught-man swears directly and positively that he heard the door open and shut but once, and if Spillane returned it should have to be opened and shut and reopened and shut again the third time to permit him egress when going to receive the gun ...

•   Gentlemen, much commentary has been and more will be made on the evidence of Coughlan, who has sworn that when he rapped up the prisoner and told him that Mr Ellis was shot he said – 'Go to the devil, he's not shot'; but we all know – everyone knows that that is a kind of exclamation that country people are fond of making, but it does not amount to an admission of guilt. It is merely an uncouth exclamation of surprise, and nothing hostile to the prisoner can be extracted from it. It has been said that Daniel did not speak to Coughlan, and it is therefore inferred that he was not within.

Rolleston recapitulated on the evidence favourable to the accused by their sister Kitty and Mary Callaghan, the 'Connaughtman's' wife. He also dealt with the evidence procured by eavesdropping and cast an aspersion on the conduct of the RMs Goold and Jones.

• I always thought that before a person was put on trial he had a right – a perfect, undoubted, legitimate right – to see the case that was to be made against him and that nothing should be held from him to prevent him from preparing for his defence, but that which has taken place in this trial would tend to lead men astray, and convince them that I was wrong in holding such an opinion, for see what occurred!

A witness has been produced for the Crown, and he has given his evidence for the Crown, but those functionaries, who were long aware of that man's evidence have, in their zeal to do justice to the Crown, been guilty of injustice to the prisoner, for this witness's evidence they have kept in their breasts, in order to snap a hanging on the prisoner.

The reported 'sensation in court' at this point was presumably due to the rarity of such an allegation against those who were normally accusers and perhaps also due to the forceful language used.

Yes, gentlemen, they have concealed the evidence from the prisoner. That evidence I should have in my brief, to enable me to defend my client before the ignominious death which awaits him if you can consign him to death upon the demoniacal evidence sworn against him by the approver and Burke; but how can he defend himself? How can I defend him, when that evidence – the evidence of the eavesdropper – is kept back until the very moment when he is placed in the position of a witness.

I denounce the conduct of the stipendiaries [the resident magistrates] who knew of this evidence but who withheld it. What good is an Act of Parliament which pretends to protect the accused when stipendiaries can act in this manner, and at their mere will and pleasure turn a solemn act of the legislature into a pretence, or, to use the graphic language of a high legal authority, transform it into a mockery, a delusion, and a snare (sensation).

… they were defeated and could not procure evidence upon which to hang a dog until this Sadleir's evidence was given.[5]

Rolleston had at least the thrust of not just one act of parliament but two to back his high indignation. There was specific provision since 1836 to supply a prisoner with copies on demand of the written depositions which arose from the examination of witnesses by magistrates. There was furthermore a competence on the part of the judge to postpone the trial if such copies had not been previously received by the accused. Sharp practice, such as seems to have been used by Gore Jones and Sadleir in this case, could perhaps have circumvented the law by not putting Sadleir's information in the form of a written deposition. An 1851 statute repeated the entitlement to copies of any depositions upon the payment of a fee. Both acts may have been flawed in seeming to concentrate on depositions taken before the accused was committed for trial.[6]

Rolleston's plea on behalf of his clients concluded by calling on the jury

to acquit the prisoners, whom he defied the jury to convict on the foul and demoniacal testimony of that polluted wretch whose very breath tainted like a pestilence the pure and balmy air of heaven.

THE JUDGE'S SUMMARY

Following a day-long barrage of multi-stranded information, capped by Rolleston's 'powerful speech', one can visualise hushed and rapt attention paid to Judge Keogh as he commenced his address to the jury. The *Nenagh Guardian* report summarised it as follows:

His Lordship complimented the jury on the strict attention they had paid to the details of the trial, and it was a matter of gratification to him that they had done so, because if during the progress of his observations upon the evidence he omitted anything which they might consider of importance, they would be able to direct his attention to it.

They should approach the consideration of the case as free as human nature can be from all prejudice, heat, or passion whatever. It was excusable for any counsel defending prisoners to show zeal, to display anxiety, and to exhibit, if they would, passion in the advocacy of their client's cause, and all this was more than excusable in counsel entrusted with the defence of the life of a human being; but a juror should divest himself of all those feelings, and should come to the consideration of the evidence free from all feelings except that which would guide him to a conscientious and just conclusion on the case – such a conclusion as would enable him in his last moments, when about to meet face to face the Almighty and eternal Judge of all, to thank God that he had discharged his duty like an honest and honourable man.

INNOCENT UNTIL GUILTY

Judge Keogh now gave an impeccable account of the common law's prescription as regards the jury's attitude to the innocence or guilt of the accused. He recapitulated on this advice later, at the conclusion of his address.

... before going into an examination of the evidence he should begin by reminding the jury that in every criminal case, the prisoner at the bar is held innocent until he is pronounced guilty by the verdict of the jury. In this country suspicion fixed no guilt on any man, he must be proven guilty beyond a reasonable doubt, and until a jury could view their verdict without a doubt and in the clearest manner possible, they should consider the prisoner innocent of the offence with which he stood charged, and giving him the benefit of the doubt under which their consciences laboured, they should acquit him, and therefore when they went into their jury room on this most serious issue, namely, whether or not the lives of the prisoners at the bar should be sacrificed to the offended laws of their country; if they entertained a rational doubt about their guilt, they should acquit them, but if they had no doubt – if they clearly and satisfactorily saw their way to that conclusion which affixed the perpetration of this crime upon the prisoners – they should pronounce a verdict of guilty, totally regardless, so far as they were concerned as jurors, of the results which would follow from that verdict.

A GUIDING PRINCIPLE

Keogh's address to the jury lasted for two hours and consisted largely of a meticulous trawl through the evidence recorded in his notebook:

… commenting on each before him, and in the course of his observations, when speaking on the evidence given by Spillane, and its corroboration by Burke, he read the following, as laid down by Lord Abinger, as a principle which should act as a guide in all questions relative to corroboration in criminal cases:

'It is a practice', said Lord Abinger, 'which deserves all reverence, that judges have told jurors not to pay attention to the evidence of accomplices unless corroborated in one essential circumstance – that essential circumstance being the identity of the accused, because a man who is able to commit an offence, and has committed it, can go into all the details about it, but that is no corroboration, because it would not tend to show that the party accused committed the offence or participated in its commission'.

Judge Keogh then reviewed the evidence of Spillane and Burke, holding the latter not to be, in law, an accomplice, and putting his evidence to the jurors as corroborative of that given by the former.

And that was the crucial judgement which led to widespread and angry review.

When he came to Sadleir's evidence, Keogh probably took into account Rolleston's denunciation of the manner of producing 'the evidence of the eavesdropper', even though Keogh tackled the subject at a different angle to that of Rolleston. Keogh went further and more or less told the jury to discount it. Whether the jury took the strength of his words on board is, of course, another matter which can never be ascertained.

Evidence obtained in this way is open to comment and subject to doubt. There may be a variation in the words used, a conversation heard in this way may be incorrectly reported, and the slightest variation in or departure from the language used may alter, and we all know it would alter the sense and meaning of that conversation, and if this observation is applicable to a conversation held between persons at large, how doubly applicable may it not be to that between persons in prison under a heavy charge.

I think the putting of prisoners in situations where they may communicate with each other is extremely wrong … and is just as bad or nearly so as if the keeper of the prison engaged them in conversations and entrapped them into making declarations which would be a just ground for the learned Attorney-General to refuse sending the case before a jury at all.[7]

LEGAL ARGUMENT

The jury retired at 8.15 p.m. There then occurred an incident which was not noted in the newspaper reports, other than the *Limerick Reporter and Tipperary Vindicator*. It was very significant legally and surfaced in later newspaper debate when claims were made that an appeal could have been made on these grounds.

> … a long legal battle ensued between the learned gentlemen on both sides and the court [i.e. the judge], Mr Johnstone contending that the judge should have told the jury that Burke was an approver, and as such his evidence did not corroborate Spillane.
> Crown counsel upheld the judge's direction.
> Mr Johnstone tendered an exception to the [judge's] charge, which his Lordship refused to accept but had the jury called out and told them that if they did not believe that Burke corroborated Spillane they would not act upon his evidence. The jury then retired again.[8]

In the light of that 'long legal battle' it is impossible to understand why Keogh did not avail of a statutory provision enabling, though not compelling, him to set out any question of law arising on a trial for the consideration of the justices of the superior courts in Dublin. He had authority to grant a postponement in executing the sentence on a conviction or he could postpone the judgement itself by the jury until the question of law had been decided.[9]

The jury returned at 9.30 p.m. to convey a verdict of guilty for both prisoners, but with a recommendation to mercy. Pronouncement of sentence was deferred until the following day.

1 The name Roche does not occur in Loughmore-Castleiney RC registers.
2 *LR & TV*, 16 Mar 1858; *NG*, 17 Mar 1858.
3 *NG*, 17 Mar 1858.
4 Rolleston was technically incorrect in accusing Burke of being an accessory *before* the fact, in so far as that category specified that such a person would not have been personally present at the crime. He was also incorrect in claiming that Burke was an accessory *after* the fact, in that such involved positive assistance in the escape or harbouring of a criminal. Rolleston could very well have accused Burke of being a 'principal in the second degree', a legal concept which replaced the archaic 'accessory *at* the fact'. Such a person 'at common law has always been equally punishable with the actual doer of the deed' – Kenny's *Outlines*, pp. 112-20.
5 *LR & TV*, 16 Mar 1858. Rolleston's use of the word 'stipendiaries' is interesting, as the term was applied to English magistrates who were paid fees per item of service. The Irish RM was paid a yearly salary, increased in 1853 from the original £400 p.a. of 1836 to £500 p.a. for twenty of the country's RMs. Whether those for the two Tipperarys were among that top twenty is not clear.
6 Indictable Offences Act, 1836 (6 & 7 Wm. IV, c. 114), ss. 3, 4; Petty Sessions (Ir) Act, 1851 (14 & 15 Vic., c. 93), s. 14.
7 *LR & TV*, 16 Mar 1858; *NG*, 17 Mar 1858. Keogh's two-hour address to the jury was not unusually long. In 1846 Judge Nicholas Ball charged the jury from 12 noon to 6.40 p.m. before adjourning it to the next morning at the request of a juror.
8 *LR & TV*, 16 Mar 1858. *The Nenagh Guardian, Freeman's Journal or Tipperary Free Press* did not report the legal argument on Burke's status.
9 Criminal Law Act, 1848 (11 & 12 Vic., c. 78), ss. 1, 2.

Chapter 10

The Black Cap

In 1858 death was the punishment for persons convicted of murder. The 'creeping civilisation' in the first half century of a slightly more liberal United Kingdom of Great Britain and Ireland and its parliament had not gone as far as abolishing capital punishment. It had indeed in 1832 removed such a penalty for horse and sheep stealing, larceny of goods to the value of £5 from a dwelling house, and forgery; in 1833 for house-breaking; in 1835 for sacrilege and for letter-stealing by servants of the Post Office; in 1842 for rape, preventing a person giving evidence, and preventing the collection of rates and taxes. Parliament was to go on in 1861 to abolish that penalty for all offences except murder and high treason.[1]

The court resumed at 9.30 a.m. on Tuesday 16 March. Two cases were dealt with before William and Daniel Cormack were brought forward for sentencing. The Clerk asked if they had anything to say as to why sentence of death should not be passed. They both replied, 'we are innocent, my Lord, as the child that was born last night'. Daniel added, 'If I was going before God this moment I could declare that we didn't go outside our door that night or until eight o'clock the following morning'.

The judge then proceeded to pronounce sentence on the prisoners. He solemnly declared:

William and Daniel Cormack, I have heard the observations you have just now made and I am bound to tell you at once I place no reliance in your statement; you have been tried and found guilty of the dreadful crime of murder, after the most careful consideration of your case.

For my own part I anxiously watched the trial on both days; I turned the evidence over and over again in my mind, to see if I was in the position of a juror, ought I entertain a doubt as to your guilt, and if after this careful revolving of your case in my mind, I could see anything that would give rise to a reasonable doubt, I would have charged the jury in your favour. As I have said I turned the matter in every possible way, and looked at it in every bearing and aspect, but I could not, and I cannot entertain, a doubt as to your guilt.

Daniel Cormack: We are innocent, my Lord, as the child born last night.

Judge: I am sorry to hear you persist in such a declaration, because it proves that as yet, you feel no sorrow or regret for the crime you committed. You were in the employment of Mr Ellis, you were about his place, you received his money, and you knew his family, yet you both went out this night with Spillane and without compunction or hesitation you took away the life of your master, and you left his wife a widow, and his children orphans.

It would be idle here to talk of the stain cast on your county by this dreadful offence. It was said at the time that the people of the locality were indifferent as to the transaction, and closed their doors; so far from this being the case, quite the contrary has been proved in evidence on your trial. The inhabitants of the place rose from their beds, and alarmed the neighbourhood. Richard Coughlan, a boy not in the employment of Mr Ellis, proceeded to your house, and asked you William Cormack to get up and come to where your murdered master lay: but you appear to be the only person indifferent as to the death of the unfortunate man, and you did not.

This was a circumstance to my mind of great importance in your case.

You were convicted on the testimony of a witness, who was truthful in everything unless when influenced by you. He told all the circumstances of the murder as it occurred; but he did not tell your guilt, why? because of your presence, William Cormack, on the jury; for you did not hesitate to sit on the inquiry into the case of the death of the man, who was consigned to death by the discharge of a gun which you fired yourself.

This was hard-hitting language, but directed, it must be remembered, at two men whom he considered guilty of an atrocious crime. Continuing, he focused on the awful fate that awaited them and advised them of the spiritual support available to them in the circumstances.

I do not make those remarks to aggravate your case, or cause you more pain than you must now feel from the position in which you are placed. I will not place myself in the position of your spiritual adviser, or seek to administer to you religious instruction. That will be done by the clergyman who will be in attendance upon you to the day of your death; and I am bound to tell you that the day is not remote, and cannot be.

The law, however, is more merciful than you were, for you did not give your unfortunate victim time to ask forgiveness of his God. You sent his soul into the presence of his Maker without affording a moment's notice. This you did without emotion or remorse, and you consigned your master to death on the highway like a dog; but the law will give you time to reflect, and you will have the assistance of clergymen, who will, doubtless, attend to you with that zeal and fidelity which people in your position always receive from their order. To their advice and teaching I commit you. ...

It often occurred that the person in whom the murderer placed the most implicit confidence was the first to turn and give evidence against him. It might even be a near relation, or a close kinsman, but, no matter who it was, someone would discover and the murderer would be brought to a ignominious end. ... In the present case the unfortunate men before me were partly convicted on the evidence of Spillane – that abominable wretch – who was as guilty as they were, but without him there would be sufficient, abundant proof to establish their guilt – and perhaps the evidence would be clearer without his testimony at all.[2]

While Keogh's reiteration of his poor opinion of the accomplice-turned-Crown witness, Timothy Spillane, is comprehensible, his comment that there was sufficient evidence to convict without him is not. The *Nenagh Guardian* report continued the judge's address in summary.

His Lordship then told the prisoners that there was no hope for them in this life. They had had a fair and impartial trial – they were defended by counsel of surpassing ability and great talent, and never did he hear a defence better conducted than in their case. They also had the advantage of a respectable and intelligent jury, who paid the greatest attention to their case to the close, and who showed their desire to save their lives by recommending them to mercy, but they should find them guilty.

There was no use, therefore, in these protestations of innocence; they could not serve them in this life, they would be very injurious to them in the world to come. But he would not dwell further on this painful subject, and though he (the Learned Judge) felt the deepest pain himself in the position in which he was then placed, and would willingly shrink from the discharge of the solemn duty that devolved upon him, yet he must pronounce the sentence of the law.

His lordship, who at this stage was deeply affected, put on the black cap, and passed sentence of death in the usual form, naming Tuesday 11 May as the date of execution.

Prior to 1836 there was a statutory obligation to carry out the sentence of death on the next day but one after the sentence, unless of course that day fell on a Sunday. There was in that era an obligation on the condemned man's gaolers to allow him a diet of bread and water only in the interim, and 'no other food or liquid'.[3]

The awesome wording of the death sentence was a standard one as follows (with names and dates inserted):

The sentence of the law therefore is that you [William Cormack and Daniel Cormack] be taken from the place where you now stand to the gaol, and from thence to the place of common execution and there on [Tuesday 11th May] be hanged by the neck until you are dead and that your body be afterwards buried within the precincts of the gaol and may the Lord have mercy on your soul.[4]

The *Nenagh Guardian* reporter noted

that during the passing of the sentence the prisoners continued unmoved, maintaining the same apparent indifference that they had showed all through since the commencement of the trial, and, as they were about being removed from the dock, Daniel turned round, and in a firm tone, addressing the court said:

Death is to us most welcome, my lord. We are as innocent as the child unborn.

The only relation of the prisoners in court, we believe, was the sister, who appeared as a witness for the defence on the trial, and her presence in the hall, where she stood bitterly but silently weeping for the fate of her unfortunate brothers, as the crowds which thronged the building left, excited the deepest commiseration and pity of all who saw her.[4]

NOTES
1   John, Earl Russell, *The English Government and Constitution* (1865 edition), p. lxii; 'Creeping Civilisation', pp. 11-14 of Donal A. Murphy, *The Two Tipperarys* (Nenagh 1994) gives a potted digest of social and economic liberalisation and development as they impacted on the Irish counties.
2   *NG*, 17 Mar 1858.
3   6 & 7 Wm IV, c. 30, 1836, repealed the quoted statute, Offences against the Person Act, 1828 (9 Geo. IV, c. 31).
4   *NG*, 5 Aug 1843, 6 April 1844.
5   *NG*, 17 Mar 1858.

County of Tipperary North Riding

A RETURN of Convicts under ~~Rule~~, ~~Entry~~, ~~or~~ Sentence of Death : at a General Assizes held in and for the North Riding of said County, commencing on Friday the 19th day of March 1858

(Pursuant to 17 & 18 Victoria, Cap. 76, Sec. 27.)

Name.	Age.	Crime.	Sentence.	Date of Conviction.	Before whom Tried.	Where Tried.	Remarks.
Daniel Cormack	23	Murder of John Ellis	To be Hanged on Tuesday the 11th day of May 1858 and their Bodies to be buried within the precincts of the Gaol	15th March 1858	The Right Honorable Mr. Justice Keogh	Nenagh	
William Cormack	26						

Dated this 19th day of March 1858

Peddar Carmichael
Clerk of the Crown for the County of Tipperary.

This Death Case, as it was termed, was signed by the Clerks of the Crown for Co. Tipperary, Henry Peddar and James Carmichael.

74

Chapter 11
Can the Death Sentence be Undone?

In 1858 there was no tribunal available to review evidence in a criminal trial and thence to consider reversing, on grounds of error of *fact*, the decision of a jury. The decision could be reviewed on the grounds of error of *law*. This could be done either by way of case stated by the presiding judge, or by way of appeal which had to be in the form of a writ of error that required the consent of the Attorney-General. Appeals were heard by the Queen's Bench, one of the superior courts at Dublin's Four Courts.[1]

Of the seventeen persons executed in Nenagh only three had an appeal heard. They were Patrick Rice and Patrick Hayes, convicted of involvement in the murder of Patrick Clarke, and William Fogarty for the attempted murder of the slate quarry manager. That 1846 appeal was by writ of error on the claim that jurors were not summoned at least six days before the first day of the court as required by the statute.[2]

Judge Keogh, as referred to in Chapter 9, did not exercise his right to state a case on the Cormacks. Whether Attorney-General Whiteside would have given his *fiat* or consent to an appeal, being in a situation of conflict with his interest as chief prosecutor, is only a matter of speculation. Amidst the commentary widespread after the execution one newspaper proffered a question as to why there was no such appeal on behalf of the Cormacks. It referred to the incident where Counsellor Johnstone tendered exceptions' to that part of the judge's charge to the jury which ruled that Burke was not an accomplice. The writer said that, notwithstanding the Attorney-General's argument and formal protest against it, the judge yielded to Johnstone, recalled the jury and re-charged them. The writer went on to say that in his opinion Judge Keogh 'acted erroneously' and in so doing closed the avenue for an appeal because the grounds for 'exception' were removed.[3]

There was only one avenue left to save the condemned men from hanging on 11 May. That was the appeal to mercy. The royal prerogative of mercy was exercisable in Ireland in 1858 by the Queen's viceroy, Lord Eglinton.

As already mentioned, the dissolution of parliament in February 1858 had brought personnel changes in the political offices of the Irish administration. However, Thomas A. Larcom, Under Secretary, being a permanent civil servant, continued in that office. A week after pronouncing the death sentence, on 25 March, Judge William Keogh, writing to Larcom in relation to another case, concluded his letter with some interesting remarks:

I have also to request that you will inform His Excellency that in the case of Daniel Cormack and William Cormack at present under the sentence of death in the Gaol in Nenagh, having been found guilty of the murder of Mr Ellis and to be executed on the 11th of May no reasons were publicly assigned [for the recommendation to mercy] but I ascertained from some of the Jury that they considered there was reason to believe that the Murder had been committed to revenge the seduction of one if not of both the sisters of the prisoners. There was evidence in the case and produced by the Crown to justify this supposition, though not at all sufficient to establish the fact. I have however requested information from the Crown solicitor and when I obtain it, should His Excellency so wish, I will submit for his perusal my notes of the evidence with any observations that occur to me. [3]

Larcom replied to him on 14 April stating that the Lord Lieutenant had now received a memorial on behalf of the Cormacks and that he would receive 'any communication you may think proper to him'. On 3 May Keogh sent on 'the papers in the case of the Cormacks ... with my report for the consideration of His Excellency'.[4] As the date appointed for the execution was fast approaching, the lapses of time, twenty days and nineteen days respectively, in the Larcom-Keogh and Keogh-Larcom responses are noteworthy.

NEWSPAPER SUPPORT

Immediately after the conviction, the *Limerick Reporter & Tipperary Vindicator*, an avowedly nationalist organ, commenced a campaign aimed at influencing the outcome of any memorial for reprieve.[5] Each issue of the paper debated aspects of the evidence, the addresses of the prosecuting and defence counsels, and the judge's charge to the jury.

In particular, the newspaper queried the ruling that Thomas Burke was deemed not to be an accomplice. The paper focused on contradictions between his evidence at the inquest and that at the trial; if the latter were true, he 'laid the snare for the unhappy Mr Ellis and drove him into the mouth of death. Why the learned [judge] did not direct the jury that this Burke was an accomplice in a primary degree, is we think a mistake to which the ablest functionaries are liable'.[6]

Correspondence in other newspapers also attempted to undermine the verdict. The *Freeman's Journal* had a letter signed M. and the *Dublin Evening Post* one signed M.M. – there are some indications that they were from the same person.[7] M. recapitulated the evidence and quoted Abinger, as had Judge Keogh, to show that approver Spillane's evidence as to the identity of the murderers had to be corroborated. He went on to attack Burke's eligibility for that role, first maintaining that the 'jury should have been told that the evidence to corroborate Spillane should be "unexceptionable", "unimpeachable" evidence. Such is manifestly the meaning of the rule, and so it will be found laid down in the books on evidence and the criminal law by Russell, Starkie and Phillips'. On those grounds Burke did not qualify, because he did not forewarn Ellis and because he swore at the inquest that he did not know who committed the murder: 'thus the murderer was corroborated by the perjurer ... no kind or degree of criminality can so effectively unfit a criminal for the witness box as perjury'.

M. M. went further. 'Have we no cause to think Burke an accomplice? An accomplice in law is "a person who is privy to, or aiding in, the perpetration of some crime; and is applied to such accessories as are admitted to give evidence against fellow criminals."' M. M. concluded, principally because of Burke's alleged foreknowledge of the murder, that he was an accomplice.

M. M. also questioned the possibility of 'this timid youth to see and discern' all the details of the murder scene at 11 o'clock on a night 'which was not moonlight'. M had a similar claim, because 'by looking at the Almanac the moon was exactly five days old'.

M. M. concluded: 'The testimony of Burke, then, is not credible and it is to be feared he is an accomplice in this horrible deed with parties yet unknown to the law'. His conclusion followed an assertion that the Cormacks had no motive to kill their benefactor, but everything to lose by his death. He dismisses 'the story of their sister's shame' because it 'was doubtingly spoken of only for a few days, and was never credited; and it is fully two years since this groundless surmise passed away'.

One issue of the *Limerick Reporter & Tipperary Vindicator*, having quoted some comments of the *Daily Express* who lauded the conviction, concluded thus:

There was one advantage which the public enjoyed during the late Administration and that was freedom, in a great measure from 'jury packing'. The onerous words 'stand by' were seldom heard in a court of justice during any Liberal Administration since the days of the illustrious Irishman, Sir Michael O'Loghlin. How many times the words were uttered at the late Nenagh assizes we shall not say; nor in reference to whom they were uttered, many of them of high station; but certain it is that Catholic gentlemen of character, of intelligence, or rank, were set aside and the juries for the trials of Catholics were composed of men, with two or three exceptions, exclusively Protestant and of the ascendancy party throughout. This is plain fact.[8]

PETITIONS
Within five weeks of the Ellis murder trial the Lord Lieutenant received a number of memorials/petitions seeking a reprieve from the death sentence for William and Daniel Cormack. They came from the members of the jury that convicted them; from the prisoners themselves, witnessed by Rev. John Scanlan, the gaol chaplain; and one initiated by Most Rev. Patrick Leahy, Archbishop of Cashel & Emly, and signed by numerous clergy, farmers, merchants, and members of the legal and medical professions.[9]

The following extracts from the petitions show the absolute significance of the judge's ruling that Thomas Burke was not an accomplice and that accordingly his evidence was admissible as corroborating that of Timothy Spillane. They also confirm, unequivocally, that the 'personal revenge' theory put forward as the motive by John Gore Jones when reporting Ellis's murder to Dublin Castle in October 1857, and alluded to in Judge Keogh's letter, was central in the charge brought against the Cormacks.

The Petty Jury's Petition
The very fact that a petition was drawn up and circulated among the members of the petty jury which found the Cormacks guilty and signed by all of them is impressive in itself. It was forwarded by Horatio Lloyd, foreman, from Mount Frisco, Dunkerrin, Roscrea, on 15 April 1858.[10]

• That in the conscientious discharge of the duty imposed on them your memorialists were obliged so to convict, the Learned Judge having told them, that Thomas Burke the corroborating Witness was a credible one, and not an Accomplice or Approver.

• That Your Memorialists concurred in a recommendation to mercy, which was given to the Learned Judge by the Foreman, on the grounds that the crime was committed, as the evidence proved, on account of the Prisoners' sister Kitty Cormack having been seduced and ruined by said Mr. Ellis. That such was the motive and the only one proved by the Crown.

The Condemned Men's Petition
An undated petition, signed with the mark of William and Daniel Cormack and witnessed by Rev. John Scanlan, Nenagh, R.C. Chaplain to the County Gaol, was received in the Chief Secretary's Office on 27 April 1858. Understandably, William and Daniel made no reference to their sister in their petition, concentrating on technicalities and contrasting the 'tainted

evidence' put forward by the Crown with the 'unimpeachable' evidence given on their behalf. Though again declaring their innocence, they were prepared, as the last paragraph shows, to acccept a prison sentence, unjust though it might be, should their lives be spared.

• That the evidence adduced upon the second trial was principally the same as that brought forward upon the first when the Jury disagreed and rested chiefly upon the testimony of an approver Timothy Spillane described by the Learned Judge in his charge as a most diabolical villain and for whose testimony memorialists refer to the notes of said Learned Judge.

• That the next important evidence was that of Thomas Burke a boy who was in the service of the said John Ellis and drove the car upon the night in question and on whose evidence said Learned Judge told the Jury the whole case against your memorialists hinged and who stated in the hearing of Stipendiary Magistrate [Jones] and without being contradicted that he was told he should rot in Gaol unless he swore against your memorialists and who on his own showing admitted he had a guilty knowledge of the intended murder for weeks before and if his evidence was at all true must have known it was to be perpetrated that very night and yet gave no intimation thereof to his master and who your memorialists are advised and submit was in the common acceptation of the term an approver also.

• That he also admitted in his cross-examination he had been guilty of willful and corrupt perjury on the Inquest and had then distinctly sworn he did not see the men who committed said murder at all and had not been in any house on the night in question after he had left his mistress to go for his master.

• That beside said Spillane and Burke there was not sufficient evidence on which a Jury could properly convict your memorialists as the Learned Judge stated and yet on evidence so tainted with crime and admitted perjury your memorialists were found guilty with a recommendation of the said Jury to mercy.

It has to be pointed out here that Judge Keogh said no such thing. In fact his address to the jury stated that without Spillane (but, by implication, taking account of Burke's evidence) 'there would be sufficient, abundant proof to establish their guilt'.

• That the other corroboratory evidence was that of the Bridewell Keeper of Thurles who deposed to conversations between your memorialists in their cells when close prisoners and which were if true to the full extent he stated (which your memorialists positively deny) did not bear the meaning attributed to them.

• That John Callaghan was also produced as a witness to swear he heard the door of memorialists open and shut at the time said Spillane stated he and your memorialists left the house to commit the crime but which would even if true which memorialists deny be equally consistent with the admitted guilt of Spillane himself and his leaving their house at the time he stated alone.

• That in order to procure a conviction the magistrates who took the evidence of said Sadlier [the Thurles bridewell keeper] and Callaghan did not take informations from them and return them to the Crown Office as was their duty as memorialists are advised and believe and therefore memorialists were unable to rebut such unexpected evidence by counter testimony.

• That the only witnesses examined by your memorialists were their sister and the wife of said Callaghan who was not under their control or subject to their examination being with the Crown witnesses in custody of the police and yet she swore, and was perfectly unimpeached, to facts entirely inconsistent with your memorialists on either of them being at the murder and returning home that night as the Crown witnesses themselves admitted that at least your memorialist William did. That such unimpeached evidence ought as they submit to counteract the tainted evidence of the Crown.

• That your memorialists are innocent of the crime imputed to them and though there may have been evidence in the case to justify a Jury legally to convict, your memorialists confidently submit it to your Excellency's cooler judgement and consideration and respectfully pray you may in the exercise of one of the highest prerogatives be pleased to commute the sentence of death passed upon your memorialists into such sentence as your Excellency may be pleased to order ...

Archbishop Leahy's Petition
The Cormacks thus had attempted to undermine the credibility of Burke and to heighten the importance of their sister's and Mary Callaghan's evidence as contradictory of her husband 'the Connaughtman's' evidence. The petition or memorial from Archbishop Leahy and co-operators again put the main focus on Burke. It re-introduced the possibility of a motive arising from land dealings which had been asserted by defence counsel Rolleston. It is also made quite clear that there was a general belief that another, known, person had committed the crime. This petition opened by revealing the hitherto undisclosed, principal reason why the jury on the trial of William Cormack failed to bring in a verdict.

• That your memorialists, having communicated with the jury who first tried the case of the Cormacks, have been informed that the causes of disagreement were numerous, but the principal ground was the view adopted by some of the jurors that they could not rely on the evidence of Thomas Burke the principal witness for the prosecution. In fact that the jury felt, and the learned judge who tried the case stated there could be no verdict against the prisoners unless the evidence of Thomas Bourke could be relied on, and considering the entire behaviour of Thomas Bourke who swore he had a knowledge amounting in the mind of any reasonable person to a certainty that his master was to be murdered and that master his benefactor and yet concealed that circumstance, who afterwards swore he did not see anyone at the time of the murder, who again swore he saw and knew the assassins of his master and yet concealed their names, and who gave no evidence until a reward appeared, that reward being of great magnitude amounting to £100 and until after (as he swore on the trial) Mr. Jones the resident Magistrate told him he would remain in Gaol until he would rot, that considering all this it was impossible to rely on him.

The memorialists suggested that it would be more natural for Thomas Burke to tell John Ellis of the murder threat as he could afford him protection. The failure to do so suggested a weakness in his character, which weakness, they speculated, led him to respond to RM Jones's alleged 'rot in gaol' threat by 'trumping up a story that would get himself out of gaol ...'.

The memorial drew attention, as did the Cormacks in their petition, to the fact that expressions in the English language used by the peasantry 'if literally construed would convey a meaning altogether different from what those using them intended'. The evidence at both trials have examples of what the Archbishop and his co-operators were referring to: 'Dan said he'd be the death of him', and a statement by one of the Cleary brothers in explaining why they left the card game early – 'they said their stepfather would kill them if they stayed'.[11]

Dealing with the crime, they placed the emphasis on the hostility generated by Ellis's actions 'in the discharge of his duties for many years past as agent to Mr Trant of Dovea and also in the management of his own property'. They expressed the view that 'no one could be persuaded that the Cormacks above all others would take away the life on whose existence their own comfort and support depended.'

Those difficulties and many others pressed on the minds of some of the jurors who first tried the case of the Cormacks and they could not agree. A second jury was impannelled and that second jury did convict the prisoners but recommended them to the mercy of the Crown.

The county-wide memorial was particularly strong in its view of the evidence obtained by John Sadleir's eavesdropping on the conversations of the Cormacks and others during their detention in Thurles bridewell. They concluded their observations on this aspect of the case thus: ' ... your memorialists most humbly protest against the principle of this practice which

81

is repugnant to the laws of this Country and unknown until adopted by the Executive of the late Government'.

Archbishop Leahy and the others here made a point similar to that in the Cormacks' own memorial – the lack of notice beforehand to the defence of certain evidence produced by the Crown. They then went on to comment on the selection of the petty jury, which was a current, contentious issue in general for quarter sessions and assizes.

• That considering the care bestowed by the High Sheriff of this county in preparing a list of fit and proper persons to serve as jurors in this county and considering the nature of the prosecution against the Cormacks which was neither of a religious, political or agrarian nature your memorialists regret the Crown solicitor thought it his duty to set aside several most respectable persons who being summoned and called attended as jurors on the occasion of the trial of the Cormacks amongst whom was a magistrate of the county [John Lenigan, Templemore], and your memorialists regret it the more as those who were set aside were exclusively Catholics which leads to the conclusion that because they were Catholics they were unfit to serve as jurors in any ordinary case.

• That your memorialists regret those causes of complaint should ever occur in the prosecution of criminal cases because they lessen that reverence due to the laws and deprive the punishment of guilt of that moral effect which all good men would wish to see it carry along with it.

INNOCENCE ASSERTED

Having dealt in great detail with the conduct of the trial and aspects of the evidence regarded as of dubious value, the Archbishop's memorial finished on a strong note. The concluding paragraphs are doubly impressive: firstly, in that the signatories, numbering eighty-one in all, could be fairly said to have their collective ear to the ground in a way that no investigating magistrates and police could; secondly, the strength of their assertion of the Cormacks' innocence. Unfortunately, it may have been an argument least weighty to a judiciary and a government executive with strong, perhaps total, faith in the judgement of a twelve-man jury.

• That altho your memorialists have felt bound to refer to those matters as they occurred in this prosecution and could not overlook them, yet it is on the ground of the total innocence of the unfortunate men who are sentenced to death that your memorialists have been induced to approach your Excellency on their behalf.

• Your memorialists beg to remind your Excellency that altho a great many men have from time to time suffered the extreme penalty of the law in the county no application of this kind was made on their behalf because their guilt was admitted by the Public who are always the most unerring judges as to the guilt or innocence of accused parties, but in this case the Public are universally satisfied beyond all doubt of the innocence of the Cormacks and that by evidence which altho it cant lead to the immediate detection of the real perpetrators yet leaves no doubt as to the innocence of those who are now awaiting the fate which ought only to fall on the guilty.

The very imposing list of signatories forms Appendix 2. It is headed by Most Rev. Patrick Leahy, Archbishop of Cashel & Emly, whose signature is over an additional plea in his own handwriting – concise and best calculated to appeal to the political figure who had both heavy responsibilities in general and now sovereign power of life and death:

I believe the case of Daniel and William Cormack now under sentence of death for the murder of Mr Ellis to be one in which, all circumstances considered, the prerogative of mercy might be most fitt[ingl]y exercised. I would, therefore, pray His Excellency, the Lord Lieutenant, to take into his merciful consideration whether the ends of justice would not on all hands be fully satisfied by a commutation of their sentence which, with seemly respect for the administration of the laws, the due protection of life, and the repression of outrage, I believe would be at once an act of mercy & of justice.

Most Rev. Daniel Vaughan, RC Bishop of Killaloe, resident in Nenagh, and Rev. James Hill Poe, Rector of Nenagh, headed a sheet of Nenagh signatures with personal messages stating their concurrence and recommending merciful consideration. The impressive list of signatures from the Thurles area was headed by Rev. John Cooney, P.P., Loughmore, and included William Kirwan, solicitor, Anthony Dwyer, merchant, Solomon Lalor Cambie, JP, and parish priests from surrounding parishes – Rev. Walter Cantwell, Cashel, Rev. Michael Banon, Moyne, and Rev. John Bourke, Moycarkey. Clonmel signatories included its Mayor, David Clancy, its Town Clerk, John Luther, Rev. Michael Burke, P.P., and William Hackett, alderman and barrister.[12]

THE LORD LIEUTENANT CONSIDERS
The question of the credibility of Thomas Burke's evidence was again placed before the Lord Lieutenant in an urgent letter sent from Nenagh on 3 May. The writer was the gaol chaplain Rev. John Scanlan.

In the case of the Cormacks under sentence of death The Learned Judge stated that the testimony of Thos. Burke the corroborating witness would not be admissible if he were an accomplice. I have this morning learned that Spillane the Approver declared to Constable Arthur of this town that Thos Burke had been an accomplice of his in the murder. As chaplain of the Gaol I think it a duty to put this fact before Your Excellency as it may be of some weight of Your Excellency's direction regarding these unhappy brothers. The Constable can be referred to. He is stationed here. ....[13]

On that date also Under Secretary Larcom sent on the reports from Judge Keogh to James Whiteside, Attorney-General, with a covering note requesting an opinion. Whiteside replied:

Upon reflection I ought not as prosecuting Col offer any opinion upon the propriety of yielding to the recommendation of the jury in Cormacks Case – the seal of counsel induces him, as his duty requires him in such a case to press for a conviction. He is not therefore the proper person to advise upon the propriety of extending or refusing mercy.

I therefore return the papers sent me and have written to Lord Eglinton [the Lord Lieutenant] to request he will consult the Chancellor [Right Hon. F. Blackburne] his proper advisor in such a case. Judge Keogh has stated the mitigating facts fairly & with his report before him the Chancellor can well advise & the Lord Lieutenant will decide.[14]

Following receipt of Whiteside's communication, Lord Lieutenant Eglinton wrote two letters to Under Secretary Larcom on 6 May, acting on Whiteside's recommendation:

I have a letter from the Attorney-General, in which he declines to give an opinion as to whether the sentence on the Cormacks should be commuted, but suggests I should take the opinion of the Chancellor.

May I therefore beg that you will arrange that he reads the case before it is sent to me, and that he sees me after I have read it – say the next morning after you forward it to me. ...

I am going out earlier tomorrow than usual & I hope you will be able to come not much after 11.

I had written to you respecting the Cormacks case just before I received your packet. I have read the portion of the case which I did not read the other day, & I return it, that you may send it at once to the Chancellor.

As the time is drawing so near, perhaps you will be kind enough to arrange with him either that he should come here between 10 & 11 tomorrow or that I should meet him at the Castle later in the day.

He will of course bring all the papers with him.[15]

It is important, at this point, to look at some key points in the summary of his charge to the jury which Judge Keogh had sent to the Under Secretary, covering Burke's status, the alleged seduction motive, and his own agreement with the verdict.

• I explained to them [the jury] the necessity that the Approver should be corroborated as a material part of the case as is the very identity of the accused & that although a jury could legally find a verdict upon testimony uncorroborated, yet that it was the duty of the judge to tell them not to do so and that they ought to act upon this recommendation. Said case for Crown hinged on Burke's testimony. I went through all the evidence minutely.

I told the jury that I did not consider Burke an approver in the eye of the law. I afterwards, at the desire of the prisoners' counsel and with the consent of the Attorney-General, explained to them that participation in the crime would constitute Burke an accomplice and told them that if they believed on the evidence that his acts brought him within the rule, his evidence, as well as that of Spillane, would require corroboration. I then directed their attention to Kate Cormack's evidence and pointed out to the jury how it would displace the case of the Crown if they could rely upon it, and on the driver of the car. I warned them if they had a rational doubt they should give the prisoners benefit of it.

• After an hour's deliberation the jury found the prisoners guilty and I did not then see, nor do I now, any reason to doubt the propriety of their verdict.

• In the verdict they made a recommendation to mercy but did not in writing assign any grounds. I however ascertained from them that it was given on the grounds stated in their Memorial to His Excellency, namely, a belief that the prisoners' sister Kitty Cormack had been seduced by Mr Ellis. As I stated in my former letter on the subject of the trial there was not evidence to establish the fact of the seduction but from all the circumstances I am disposed to concur to the belief formed by the jury that Mr Ellis had illicit consort with the prisoners' sister.

I have marked in my report the parts of the evidence for the Crown which were calculated to sustain this belief and to show how the alleged seduction influenced the conduct of the prisoners. I am not aware of any other circumstances which His Excellency, the Lord Lieutenant, might possibly consider as calculated to mitigate the character of the crime of which the prisoners have been convicted.[16]

THE ELEVENTH HOUR

Perhaps Archbishop Leahy had some feedback through a private channel that a reprieve would not be forthcoming for he made a desperate effort on Friday 7 May to influence the outcome, this time invoking the assistance of the influential Dr Paul Cullen, Archbishop of Dublin:

The case of the unfortunate Brothers Cormack, now under sentence of death for the murder of Mr. Ellis, is one in which, I conscientiously believe, all things considered, the prerogative of mercy ought be most fully expressed.

There are before the Lord Lieutenant at this moment two Memorials praying for a cummutation of sentence – one from the Jurors before whom the case was tried – the other from a large and respectable number of persons in the County Tipperary, signed by several L. Clergymen, by the Bishop of Killaloe and myself, and by some Protestant rectors.

In considering the case His Excellency will, as a matter of course, consult the Judge who tried the Cormacks – Judge Keogh.

May I ask your Grace to say a word to Judge Keogh on behalf of these poor people.

I am only afraid it is now too late, as the day fixed for the execution is the 11th Instant.[17]

Archbishop Cullen received Dr Leahy's letter that same day (7 May) and wrote immediately to a Rev. Mr O'Dwyer:

The worthy Archbishop of Cashel is anxious that a word should be said to Judge Keogh in favour of the McCormacks, who were lately sentenced to death. His Grace is of the opinion that the exercise of mercy in this case would do much good. One of the principal witnesses is also believed to have been the murderer himself and there is on that account a general desire that the lives of the poor men should be saved. Would you be so good as to say a word to the judge, who, I am sure, will say a word to the Lord Lieutenant in favour of a mitigation of sentence.[18]

Rev. O'Dwyer obviously acted immediately for, on Sunday afternoon 9 May, Judge William Keogh sent a communication from Bushy Park, Enniskerry, to Larcom:

The enclosed letters, one from Dr Cullen, the other from Dr Leahy from Cashel to him, have been this moment placed in my hands. At the risk at being considered a transgressor against official rules I send them forward for the consideration of the Lord Lieutenant as in a case of life and death I cannot keep anything back. You have already my view of the alleged seduction of the Cormacks sister. I have no doubt that Dr. Leahy feels strongly on that point and he is unlikely to move without good reasons. Excuse me again for troubling you on this subject.

An answer will reach me at the Court of Pleas up to 3 o'c tomorrow. If any change is made in the fate of the convicts of course a special messenger will be sent to Nenagh.[19]

However, Keogh's intervention was too late, as indicated by the date of [Friday] 7 May on the announcement that no reprieve was forthcoming, sent out by the Under Secretary to Thomas Rock, Governor of Nenagh Gaol:

I am to authorize that you will acquaint Daniel and William Cormack prisoners under sentence of Death in the Gaol under your charge that the Lord Lieutenant on full consideration of all the circumstances of their case has felt it to be His painful duty to leave the Law to take its course.

Dr Leahy and Keogh received similarly-worded, curt communications from Larcom, dated 7 and 10 May respectively. Leahy's included an acknowledgement of receipt of the memorial. To Keogh he added:

I am aware from my own knowledge that H.E. spared no labour or time in making himself thoroughly conversant with all the particulars.[20]

THE END OF THE LONG DAY

It would appear that up to Saturday 8 May the Cormacks were confined in cells in one of the seven cell blocks which formed the main part of the gaol, rather than in the specially-designed accommodation in the gaol gatehouse for those condemned to death. We know from RM Goold's letter of 7 April 1858 that Timothy Spillane the approver [was] '... constantly crying and loitering near the Cormacks he prosecuted'. As we will see, Spillane had departed for Limerick gaol by the date of the execution but Burke and Callaghan were still in Nenagh.

There is newspaper evidence to suggest that the Cormacks were moved on the Saturday to the vicinity of the scaffold in the gaol gatehouse.[21] Its downstairs accommodation consisted of two day rooms, and two small unroofed exercise yards surrounded by walls thirty feet high. To walk a mile needed eighty to ninety circuits of a yard. Each yard had a dry toilet. Upstairs there were four single 'death' cells, two prison warder's/turnkey's rooms, and the execution preparation room.

NOTES

1   Sir William Valentine Ball in *Encyclopaedia Brittanica,* vol. 2, p. 129d.
2   *NG*, 6 June 1846.
3   *Evening Mail*, 29 Sept 1858.
4   NLI, Larcom Papers MS 7636. Keogh's letter of 25 Mar 1858 to Larcom. Any information he may have got from the Crown Solicitor (Thomas Kemmis) has not surfaced.
5   NA, CSORP 1920/8218, Larcom to Keogh, 14 Apr; Keogh to Larcom, 3 May 1858.
6   The editor-proprietor of the *LR & TV* was Waterford-native Maurice Lenihan (1811-95). Lenihan came to Nenagh in 1841 to found a nationalist newspaper, the *Tipperary Vindicator*. He amalgamated the title with the *Limerick Reporter* when he bought that paper in 1849. The new title was published from both Nenagh and Limerick addresses.
7   *LR & TV*, 2 April 1858.
8   *LR & TV*, 16 & 20 April 1858 quoted the letters from M and M.M. in full.
9   *LR &TV*, 19 Mar 1858.
10   NA, CSORP 1920/8218.
11   *LR & TV*, 16 Mar 1858.
12   NA, CSORP 1920/8218. The reward money in the original is £1,000, obviously in error for £100.
13   NA, CSORP 1920/8218.
14   NLI, Larcom Papers MS 7636.
15   NLI, Larcom Papers MS 7636; Cormack file, Co. Library, Thurles.
16   NA, CSORP 1920/8218.
17   ditto.
18   ditto.
19   ditto.
20   ditto.
21   *NG*, 12 May 1858.

Chapter 12
'The Day Darkened'

Thomas Rock conveyed the account of the execution to Under Secretary Larcom in a manner as concise and formal as the notice of non-reprieve from Larcom had been four days previously.

I have the honour to state for your information that Daniel and William Cormack were this day Executed in front of the County Prison. And after their Execution their Bodies have been buried within the precincts of the Gaol, agreeable to the Sentence passed on them. Both have publicly declared their innocence on the drop. There was no Excitement, nor was there any great crowd assembled on the occasion. Mr FitzGerald Sub Sheriff and Mr. Flemming R.M. attended the Execution with a large Constabulary force.[1]

The *Nenagh Guardian*, which was opposed to capital punishment, described the execution on that Tuesday 11 May 1858 in a very different tone.

Shortly before 11 o'clock Gerald Fitzgerald, sub-Sheriff, entered the prison bearing the warrant of death, and immediately after 160 of constabulary, horse and foot, under the command of John Duncan, Esq., County Inspector, and Sub-Inspectors O'Dell, Fulton and Harnett, drew up in three divisions before the scaffold. John Flemming, Esq., RM, was also present. At ten minutes past eleven a procession was formed and the mournful party proceeded from the condemned cells, the prisoners attended by the clergy, the officers of the prison, and the Sheriff. Having arrived at the press room, the operation of pinioning the arms, to which the unfortunate men yielded without resistance, was performed by the executioner. This over, the door leading to the scaffold was unfolded and the prisoners, accompanied by the clergy who held crucifixes in their hands, advanced to the edge of the fatal engine. ...

The report goes on to say that William and Daniel, in turn, addressed the assembled crowd. There then followed their positioning on the trapdoors, the hooding of the heads, the placing of the noose, the springing of the lever and the drop of the bodies. The newspaper, though opposed to the punishment, seems to have indicated its agreement with the verdict by its use of the word 'culprits':

The Rev Mr Cleary then called on those present to pray for the culprits. This request was responded to by the assemblage, which did not number more than between two and three hundred people, consisting for the most part of women and children. … A special Mass for their souls was said in the Roman Catholic Chapel of this town this morning, and during the day shutters were kept up on the windows of all the Catholic shopkeepers and some three or four Protestants followed their example.[2]

After about fifteen minutes the bodies were lowered to the ground and placed in coffins for removal to the gaol burial area behind the male infirmary. This small area held the mortal remains of the other executed persons and of persons who had died while in gaol and whose relatives did not arrange for burial outside. It was not preserved when new secondary school buildings were erected in the grounds in the 1950s and now lies under a layer of tarmacadam.[3]

An account of the unusual weather which erupted after the executions has lingered in local tradition. This is verified by a report in the *Nenagh Guardian* of Saturday 15 May 1858:

At about 2 o'clock on Tuesday a fearful storm passed over this town. The day first darkened and the atmosphere became very sultry and oppressive. Soon after, the lightning began to play, and the thunder burst in fearful crashes. The rain immediately descended in torrents such as not has been seen in this place for a considerable time past, though, strange to say, a drop did not fall in some places a mile from here.

We get an intimate view of William's and Daniel's last days from a letter that appeared in that Saturday issue of the *Nenagh Guardian*. Signed by three of Nenagh's Catholic curates, Reverends George Corbett, Martin Cleary and Patrick Shannon, it was written to refute a report that the paper had carried in their Wednesday edition to the effect that Daniel Cormack 'had paid no heed to the ministrations of his clergy, maintaining to the last a deplorable indifference to his soul's welfare'. The priests' letter continued:

That sentiment is a great injustice to the memory of Daniel Cormack. So reconciled was he to his fate, that he declared on Monday, on several occasions, and in the presence of many, 'he had such confidence in the mercy of God, and was so conscious of his innocence, that he was as willing to suffer in the morning as to return home with his friends'.

Unfortunately, he heard on Monday that his sister was in town and was most urgent in his wish to see her. As his seeing her on a former occasion had a most injurious effect on him and was very near destroying his reason, it was deemed prudent, however painful, to prevent a meeting which at a critical period might be attended with a similar effect.

It is true that early on Tuesday morning he declared his mind was and would be unsettled until he had seen and taken his last leave of his sister, but when he was assured it was impossible he could see her as she had left town, he at once resumed his former good disposition, turned his attention to his God, and the salvation of his soul.

Nothing could be more edifying during the remaining hours of his life than his resignation, his confidence in the mercy of God and the fervour with which he repeated the prayers suggested on the occasion. Those who witnessed the readiness with which he left the cell when the signal was given to proceed to the place of execution, the fervour with which he exclaimed 'Lord, I come', the distinctness with which he gave the responses during the procession and his patient submission during the trying moment when he was pinioned, must have been deeply impressed with his resignation and religious feeling, as were all who heard his dying declaration and witnessed his death. ...[4]

In 1984 the Gatehouse of the former County Gaol, along with its Governor's House, was refurbished as a Heritage Centre. This development resulted in the cells where the Cormacks, and other persons condemned to death, spent their last days, being open to the public for the first time. A single cell is 7.5 feet (2.28 metres) long, 5 feet (1.52 metres) wide and 7 feet (2.13 metres) high and lit by a small window with a sloped window cill (to throw light into the room). It was guarded by a heavy cast-iron door with a ventilation/viewing panel – there is a sample on one cell in the Gatehouse.

NOTES
1   NLI, Larcom Papers MS 7636; copy in Cormack file, Co. Library, Thurles. Hanging in public was abolished by the Capital Amendment Act, 1868 (31 & 32 Vic., c. 24); henceforth execution was to take place 'within the walls of the prison'.
2   *NG*, 12 May 1858.
3   A newspaper report of 1844 has a description of the body of the executed man being lowered down and placed in a coffin. The exact location of the burial area is shown on the scale model of the County Gaol in Nenagh District Heritage Centre.
4   *NG*, 15 May 1858.

Chapter 13

Burke & Spillane

O nce the trial of William and Daniel Cormack was over the immediate concern of the authorities was to pay off the Crown witnesses, and to arrange for the emigration of Thomas Burke and Timothy Spillane to a safe country.

Firstly in relation to Burke, matters moved swiftly and smoothly. He was detained in Nenagh gaol while the arrangements were made. By 27 April the £100 reward offered by the Lords Justices was allocated by Thomas Kemmis, Crown Solicitor on the Leinster Circuit, as follows:[1]

Burke	£35
Spillane	£30
Callaghan	£15
Andrew Cormack	£10
Richard Coughlan	£10

It appears that John Burke, who was not involved in any way in the tragic incident, opted to accompany his younger brother into exile. Accordingly, he was included in all the emigration arrangements. These extended to outfitting the two and instructing the emigration agent, whose name by coincidence was Ellis, to make the passage arrangements.

Samuel Ellis duly informed Under Secretary Larcom that he had arranged 2nd class berths at £5.15s 0d each; extra provisions and bedding for £3.00 and purchased a bank draft on Quebec for £30. The latter was the balance of Burke's £35 share of the reward which he would be paid on landing in Canada. He was to get the £5 before taking off. Ellis requested that 'the parties should appear at this office at 10 o'clock on Monday morning the 17th inst ...'[2]

A fascinating document which survives from these arrangements is an estimate of the cost of outfitting the two Burkes, submitted for sanction to the Inspector-General of Police by John Duncan, County Inspector, Nenagh. Sanction was given, so presumably the purchases were made and tailoring done in Nenagh.[3]

The document shows that it was intended to spend the same amount outfitting John Burke, aged 21 years and 5' 9" tall. He was also to get £5 pocket money.

Name	Age Yrs	Height ft ins	Make	Particulars	Amount £	s	d
Thomas Burke	17	5 5	mid stout	**To cost of:**			
				2 yds of Frieze at 4s/6d a yard for coat	0	9	0
				Trimmings for do	0	2	6
				Tweed for vest & trimmings	0	3	0
				31/2 yds of cord for Trousers	0	4	6
				Hat	0	2	0
				4 Shirts made up at 2s 3d each	0	9	0
				4 Pairs of Socks at 5d a pair	0	1	8
				2 Neck ties at 9d each	0	1	6
				2 Pocket handkerchiefs	0	0	8
				Tailor for making up suit of clothing	0	7	0
				1 pair of Shoes	0	9	6
				Total	**2**	**10**	**4**

A week after William and Daniel Cormack were executed Thomas Burke began his journey into exile, alone, since his brother had by now decided against travelling. This decision sparked off another spate of correspondence between the Under Secretary and the Emigration Agent and the Crown Solicitor over recoupment of the fare and what was to happen to the outfit. Charity or convenience prevailed and the young man was let keep the new outfit and the £5. Kemmis was refunded the fare as Samuel Ellis found another passenger for the Burke booking.[4]

The first leg of Thomas Burke's journey was under police escort from Nenagh to Roscrea by hired car. He went from there by train to Dublin where he stayed overnight, and thence to Liverpool by steamer to embark on the *Mountaineer* sailing to Canada.

All went smoothly to Liverpool. Then an indiscretion on that first leg overtook him and brought 'the case of the Cormacks' back on to centre stage again.

On his return from Roscrea, Constable Arthur, Burke's police escort, reported in writing to John Duncan, County Inspector, that Burke had told himself, the car driver and sub-constable Kenny independently of each other, that the evidence he gave against the Cormacks was not true. Arthur's report was sent post haste to the Deputy-Inspector General of the Constabulary, Henry John Brownrigg, in Dublin.[5]

When this communication reached Solicitor-General Edmund Hayes on 19 May he moved rapidly on it.

I think that no time should be lost in sending a telegraphic message to Liverpool so that if possible Burke may be detained & the matter to which he referred in his communication with the carman fully investigated. Get the constables and other person to whom the telegram may be sent direct if time permits to communicate with a Magistrate and, after making a short information (if required by the Magistrate) that he has reason to believe that Burke has been guilty of wilful and corrupt perjury on the trial of the murder of Mr Ellis and is about to leave by the *Mountaineer*, seek to get a warrant for his arrest so that he may be transmitted to Ireland.

At all events even at the hazard of a slight irregularity, it is most desirable that the matter should be pushed to the bottom and that Burke if guilty should not be allowed to escape – I am without a warrant, if necessary I advise that the Constable should effect an arrest.[6]

On 19 May Dublin got a telegraph from Liverpool saying that Burke had been detained. Telegraphic instructions were sent immediately to 'bring him to Dublin without delay'.[7]

Burke was examined in Dublin by Deputy Inspector-General Brownrigg. Burke denied the allegation and within two days was on his way back to Liverpool to resume his journey to Canada.[8] No more is known of him.

Burke did indeed make such a claim – to the car driver and to his police escort independently of each other, and again to his second police escort who set up a type of enquiry in Roscrea after he heard the story from his colleague and from the driver.

In a statement made before Brownrigg, Dublin Castle, on 21 May 1858, car driver Michael Gleeson told how he drove Constable Arthur, sub-Constable Kenny and Thomas Burke from Nenagh to Roscrea 'a few days ago' [15 May].

I had a conversation with Burke. I asked him 'are you the boy who drove the gentleman who was shot' (meaning Mr. Ellis). I am says he. Well said I 'was those men in it' – meaning the Cormacks. 'Well I don't know whether they were or not' said he. Then I said 'why did you swear on the inquest you did not know those men? and why did you afterwards swear their lives away' – (meaning at the trial). He replied – I was persecuted by every one, & was told if I did not swear against them I would be transported for life. I did not ask – nor did he say – who told him so. I said I would not do it for the full of the car of money, & he said he would not wish it for all he ever seen.[9]

The statement was signed with his mark, and witnessed by J. Maunsell, a senior clerk in the constabulary ofice. Sub-Constable George Kenny also made a statement to Brownrigg on the same day:

I was with Con. Arthur escorting Burke to Roscrea. Burke asked me did I see the men hanging (was sitting on the same side of the car with Burke, and the Const on the opposite side). I said I did. I asked him if he was convenient – he replied he was at the other end of the Gaol. He then said 'If I told the truth nothing would happen the Cormacks'. In a little time after he said he did not know whether they were there or not – that he only suspected from what the Cormacks said before Mr. Ellis was shot that sooner or later they would have his life – I then told the Constable, privately at the Station House, what Burke had said. I was present when the Constable questioned him on the subject & he made the same statement.

Burke said when he was in Bridewell during the investigation of the case that from hearing 'this thing' & 'that thing', some lies & some he knew to be true, that he was afraid he would be transported if he did not say as he said.

On returning to Nenagh after leaving Burke at Roscrea, the Carman stated to me and to Const Arthur that 'Burke told him he did not know who was in it' (meaning as I believe the Cormacks) & that Burke should be hanged or transported – or words to that effect. We did not mention to the Car Driver what passed between Burke and ourselves.[10]

Constable Patrick Arthur also made a statement to Brownrigg on the same day. He said that Kenny told him:

Burke said he did not know who killed Mr. Ellis – thereupon I asked Burke if he knew who shot Mr. Ellis and he said he did not, and that if he swore the truth against the Cormacks they would not be hanged. I then asked him what was the reason he swore against them – he said people told him he would be transported. I asked him why he said the Cormacks were there, & he said he came to that conclusion from what the Cormacks had previously told him.

The general impression in the Country is that the Cormacks were not the guilty parties, suspicion is attached to a man named Burke.

The driver of the car upon this occasion, Michl Gleeson, (after I put the questions to Burke) said 'that fellow ought be transported or hanged, for, he told me he did not swear the truth against the Cormacks'.[11]

The credibility of Thomas Burke's evidence, and Judge William Keogh's ruling that it was admissible, is certainly challenged by these statements. Though the statements themselves were never made public, the next chapter will show that there was knowledge abroad as to the general thrust of the car driver's story.

Solicitor-General Hayes's decision on the matter is recorded in a memorandum placed on file by him on 21 May, the same day as the statements were made in Dublin Castle by the car driver and the two policemen. He set out fully the rationale which governed his decision.

Upon reading the report of the 17th May I felt most anxious that the person who gave reason to suppose that he had by false swearing illegally achieved the death of a fellow creature should not be allowed to escape. With that view I directed his apprehension & also that the cardriver and members of the Constabulary force mentioned in the report should be produced as witnesses. I have read the deposition of the prisoner's [T. Burke] statement taken under the careful superintendence of Mr Brownrigg. I have also very carefully read the learned judge's notes of the trial and after the whole I am of opinion
1   That there is no case sufficient to send Burke for trial on a charge of wilful and corrupt perjury.
2   That as far as I can judge there is no probability of any further evidence being obtained which may warrant a magistrate in the so doing.
3   That there is a very good reason to believe that notwithstanding the statement of Burke, the cardriver and the constables (which statements I believe to have been made) the evidence given by Bourke at the trial was substantially true. And that the end of justice in the punishment of the guilty had been attained.
Entertaining those views I believe Burke ought not to be longer detained and that he ought to be sent back to Liverpool to proceed on his intended voyage if he so desires it.[12]

News of Burke's arrest in Liverpool was broken by the *Dublin Evening Post* on 20 May. Though short on detail, nevertheless it was sensational. The *Packet* of 25 May claimed to have learned the 'full facts' but, while their account of the steps taken tally with the official documents, they too were short on detail. The *Daily Express*, described by the *Dublin Evening Post* 'as the official journal of the Irish Government', carried a brief, but informed, account of the incident, concluding that Burke's statement to the car driver was found to be groundless and 'given with a view to stand well with the people'[13]

These words appear nowhere in the formal account of Burke's interrogation, which was as follows.

Thomas Burke – Being fully cautioned, states, I was in the employment of the late Mr Ellis. I was driving his car the night he was shot. I was examined at the trial of the Cormacks. I saw the man who shot him. I was about two yards from him. I knew the man – Billy Cormack was the man – I saw Tim Spillane & Daniel Cormack there at the same time about a yard and a half behind Dan – partly at the right hand side. I knew Const Arthur and Sub Constable Geo. Kenny by sight. They escorted me on a Car recently from Nenagh to Roscrea. I persist in saying I saw Bill Cormack fire the shot that night, and Spillane & Dan Cormack with him.

It is clear from the following that Deputy-Inspector Brownrigg, who had the powers of an examining magistrate by virtue of his rank in the constabulary, read the depositions of Gleeson, Arthur and Kenny to Burke. He obviously asked him at each point to confirm or deny the various statements quoted.

• The Car Driver asked me 'if I was the boy who was with Mr Ellis the night he was shot. Was I Burke'? I answered 'I was'. He then said 'the boys said they died innocent'. I replied 'I did not know that'. I meant by that, that I did not believe what he said – that they died innocent. He said 'I wronged them' – I did not mind what he said. At this time the Constable and sub-Constable were walking behind the car, and I was sitting on the car with the driver. The car driver asked me 'were those men in it'. I said they were. After that I said 'I did not know whether they were or not' made that answer because I did not wish to be talking to him.

Nothing more passed until we got to Roscrea station. Heard the car driver inform a Porter there who I was, & that I swore the lives of the Cormacks away. The car driver did not ask him why he swore at the inquest they were not there. Is quite sure of this. At Roscrea station the driver said to the Porter 'was not he a dangerous fellow to swear those men's lives away'. I said nothing in reply.

I did not say to the car driver that 'I was persecuted or was afraid I would be transported for life'. Nobody told me so. No one persecuted me. I was told I would be left in the Gaol until I would rot if I did not tell all I knew – Mr Gore Jones told me this. The car driver said 'he would not wish to be in my Coat for the full of the Car of money'. I made no reply that I recollect. I do not recollect I said 'I would not wish it for all I ever saw'.

Having given an explanation for the contradiction between his and car driver Gleeson's accounts of one point and a flat denial of another, he was now directed to the statements of the two policemen. He produced a contradiction, three denials, and two pleas of failure to recollect aspects of Arthur's statement. He followed this with a loss of recollection and three flat denials apropos Kenny's statement.

• I know Constable Arthur now present by eye-sight. He was one of the escort on the car with me. I had no conversation with the Constable about this matter until I went to the Roscrea Station. I cannot recollect the questions asked me by the Constable. The Constable asked me 'if I knew the man who shot Mr Ellis'. I said 'I did'.

I did not say to the Constable that 'I did not know who shot Mr Ellis & that if I swore the truth against the Cormacks they would not be hanged'. It was not to the Constable I said that. I did not say it to any one. The other Constable – Kenny –

97

said to Arthur and to me ' if I swore the truth now would the Cormacks be hanged' I said 'they would': as far as I recollect this is what I said. I did not say to the Constable people told me I would be transported.

I do not think the Constable asked me 'if I knew the Cormacks were there'. I did not say 'I came to the conclusion they (the Cormacks) were there from what they told me before.'

• I know Sub-Const Geo. Kenny by sight. He was one of the escort with Arthur. I had a conversation with Kenny who asked me 'was I sure the Cormacks shot Mr Ellis.' I said 'I was' – Kenny said 'it was not true – that they would not tell a lie before going before their God'. I do not recollect anything more. I did not ask Kenny 'if he saw the men hanging' but he asked me, and I said 'I did not'.

I do not think I told the Sub-Constable that 'if I told the truth nothing would happen the Cormacks.' I am quite sure I said nothing of the kind. I did not tell Kenny that 'I did not know whether they were there or not – that I only suspected from what the Cormacks said before Mr Ellis was shot that sooner or later they would have his life'. I don't think I told him this. I did not tell Kenny that 'from hearing this thing & that thing, & some lies & some truth that I was afraid I would be transported'. Constable Kenny asked me 'was I frightened or anything about it. I said 'I was': that 'they were telling things of me that was not true – then I told the truth to save myself'.

The statements of Constable Arthur, Sub-Constable Kenny & Michael Gleeson having been read for me, I state they are not true.

    his
Thos X Burke
    mark
Acknowledged before me this 21 May 1858
Truly read and witnessed by me
J Maunsell [Senior Clerk]   J H Brownrigg[14]

This whole episode, centred on a garrulous Burke – whether speaking from partial contrition or from lying bravado 'with a view to stand well with the people' – brought the awful probability that the Cormacks had been wrongly hanged into the media again. It received coverage in the *Waterford News*, *Tipperary Examiner*, the *Packet*, *Dublin Evening Post* and the *Evening Mail*. Supporters campaigned for a full disclosure of the facts by the government, with the *Limerick Reporter & Tipperary Vindicator* particularly strong on the subject.[15]

In July 1858 George Goold, RM, Clonmel, wrapped up the local end of the 'case of the Cormacks' regarding the Crown witnesses with the submission of an account detailing the extra expenditure incurred since the trial and which was the responsibility of the exchequer.[16]

Name of Witness	Period	Days detained	Total
1) Timothy Spillane	16/3/58-20/4/58	35 days @ 2/6d	£4 -7 -6
2) Thomas Burke	16/3/58-15/5/58	60 days @ 2/6d	£7-10-0
3) John Callaghan	16/3/58-22/5/58	66 days @ 2/6d	£8-5-0

It is noteworthy that John Callaghan, the Cormacks' lodger, was detained in custody for over two months after the trial – presumably for his safety. As with Burke, no more is known of him.

SPILLANE

Timothy Spillane's behaviour in Nenagh gaol after the trial and conviction of the Cormacks was causing concern. This gave rise to RM Goold writing to Dublin on 7 April 1858 urging his removal. Goold quoted Governor Thomas Rock as stating that, unless immediate steps were taken

he [Spillane] may injure himself or some of the prison officers whom he has assaulted... in an effort to get away. He is most outrageous at being kept locked up and long swears that he will destroy himself. ... He is most unpleasant and constantly crying and loitering in the area of the Cormacks he prosecuted, but it is nothing to the way he is treated by you [Goold] and Mr Jones keeping him here.[17]

He was duly transferred to Limerick gaol on 20 April 1858, causing the *Limerick Reporter & Tipperary Vindicator* to comment some months later, 'that terrible monster, Spillane, is sunning himself every day outside the police barracks in William Street where his *locus standi* is at present'.[18]

Spillane was scheduled to give evidence in Nenagh courthouse at the summer assizes of 1858 against Patrick Maher. That case arose from Spillane's statement that Maher owned the gun used to kill Ellis. Maher was arrested and charged with conspiracy to murder Lieut-Col. William Knox, Brittas, Thurles. However, as his trial was postponed Dublin duly approved that Spillane be 'supported and protected at the public expense until after the next spring assizes'. At the same time steps were put in motion, through Samuel Ellis, Emigration Agent, to arrange his passage out of the country and pay '£7 on landing'.[19]

In fact Spillane never appeared again as a witness, for at the spring assizes of 1859 the court was told that there would be no trial and Patrick Maher was discharged by proclamation.[20] This cleared the way for Spillane's release after almost eighteen months in protective custody.

In April 1859 a request was sent by George Goold, RM, through Thomas Kemmis, Crown Solicitor on the Leinster Circuit, to the Constabulary Office in Dublin Castle, to the effect that 'Spillane be allowed to see his family before emigrating to Canada'. Kemmis considered the request 'a reasonable one'. He went on:

Spillane is now under the protection of the police at Limerick and his father (who is a policeman) and his family are in Ardfert in the Co. of Kerry. I have spoken to Sir Henry Brownrigg and he thinks Spillane may be sent in charge of a steady policeman in plain clothes to Ardfert and allowed to remain for three or four days, authorities to pay the expenses.[21]

This is the only evidence found that Canada was to be Spillane's destination. Emigration agent Samuel Ellis was paid £6 15s 0d on 29 April 1859 for arranging his passage but the trail ends there.[22]

NOTES

1   NA, CSORP 1920/8218, No. 13731.
2   ditto, No. 13931. Has 'to pay' written across it.
3   ditto, No. 13810. There were ten tailors in Nenagh per Slater's Directory of 1856. But a tailor serving a gaol sentence might also have made them.
4   NA, CSORP 1858, No.s 14181 & 14244.
5   NA, CSORP 1920/8218, No. 59706. Co. Inspector John Duncan sent it on to Brownrigg, who passed it to the Solicitor-General.
6   ditto, No. A59706.
7   NA, CSORP 1920/8218.
8   ditto, No. 14386.
9   NA, CSORP 1920/8218.
10   ditto.
11   ditto.
12   ditto, No. 14386.
13   *DEP*, 20 May 1858.
14   NA, CSORP 1920/8218.
15   *LR & TV*, 21 May 1858; *Daily Express* 24 May 1858; *DEP*, 25 & 27 May 1858; *Packet*, 25 May 1858.
16   NA, CSORP 1920/8218, No.s 15895, 15899, 150199.
17   ditto, No. 13224.
18   *LR & TV*, 26 May 1858.
19   *NG*, 20 July 1858; NA, CSORP 1859, No.16685.
20   *NG*, 19 Mar 1859.
21   NA, CSORP 1920/8218, No. 4403. Brownrigg, who was knighted in 1858, was now Inspector-General, having succeeded McGregor in that year – Séamus Breathnach, *The Irish Police* (Dublin 1974), p. 46.
22   NA, CSORP 1859, No.s 3273, 3762, 3909, 4403.

Chapter 14
'Only a couple of Tipperary peasants'

1. ON THE STREET

On 13 May, the Thursday after the Cormacks were executed, the RM, John Gore Jones, and sub-Inspector Burke had to call out the constabulary to quell what could have developed into a serious incident in Thurles. Being a church holyday, there was a large number of people in the town. In the afternoon a crowd gathered and displayed riotous behaviour outside the shop of James Knaggs, a Protestant shopkeeper.

They spoke freely of the Cormacks and expressed firm belief in their innocence. A few weeks later a crowd gathered outside the courthouse during a petty sessions at which RM Jones was presiding and disrupted proceedings with loud groans.[1]

Another incident on 25 May involved John Sadleir, the bridewell keeper, who was to be haunted for some time by reverberations of aspects of his role in the detention of the Cormacks. The newspaper report stated that, as Sadleir

was passing the house in the town where the Cormacks' sisters reside, they came out and began to abuse him. They attracted a crowd, composed for the most part of women and children, who followed him and conducted themselves in so menacing a manner that he found it necessary to draw a pistol in order to deter them from using actual violence against him. He managed to keep them at bay until a party of police came to his assistance and safely escorted him to his abode.[2]

These incidents, and growing tensions in the town, led grand juror John Trant, Dovea, to apply to Dublin on 17 June seeking police protection for himself and extra police for Thurles. The reply to his first request was that 'a mounted man could be spared' or that alternatively 'two dismounted men could be made available on Mr Trant agreeing to pay one shilling a night for each'. The answer to his second request was: 'I should think that an increase of the force in Thurles might be dispensed with at present'.[3]

In the newspapers of late May and early June the list of judges for the summer assizes named William Keogh for the Connaught circuit. He never again presided at a Tipperary North Riding assizes in Nenagh.

The 'case of the Cormacks' was raised in the House of Commons on four occasions in June-July 1858 – once by Dr John Brady, Liberal MP for Leitrim, and on three occasions by Daniel O'Donoghue, The Glens, Co. Kerry, commonly known as The O'Donoghue. He was MP for Co. Tipperary as of March 1857 when he secured the seat in a by-election.[4] All four questions were addressed to James Whiteside, MP, Attorney-General for Ireland, and, of course, who had led the prosecution case against the Cormacks.

Whiteside, forewarned by John Bagwell, the Clonmel-based Conservative MP for Tipperary, that Bagwell intended to ask a question, 'he says – in no unfriendly spirit', about Thomas Burke, wrote to Under Secretary Larcom for details of the investigation.

Now he [Bagwell] thinks we could now well answer his question and so remove false impressions from the public mind without sharing what did actually take place respecting Burke since the trial. There never in my opinion was a clearer case than in this same case.[5]

Whiteside wrote again to Larcom on 1 June: 'Your packet relating to Burke arrived just in time, as Mr Brady has anticipated Bagwell and put the question. You will see the report in the papers tonight.'

Brady asked whether there was any truth in what was appearing in the Irish newspapers about Burke having confessed to giving false evidence under coercion, whether this had been investigated, and what had happened to Burke.

Whiteside made light of the question, saying he believed no such confession had been made but that it had been alleged. He conceded that it had been reported to the government that Burke had made a statement to the driver of the car. His colleague in Dublin, he said, had responded and made an enquiry into the matter but found there was nothing in it. He did not know where Burke now was, and if government knew they would not disclose it.[6]

The following paragraph in that letter from Whiteside to Larcom on 1 June also gives a very revealing insight into the mental attitude of an Attorney-General who was implicitly condemning the action of his own Solicitor-General in bringing back Burke for interrogation. He was also in effect discounting the possibility of a witness ever being brought to book for a prima facie case of perjury after the conclusion of a trial. And Whiteside here disregarded his other role as prosecutor, although he had carefully distinguished between the two roles when asked by the Lord Lieutenant to advise on the substance of the case at the time the memorials for reprieve were being considered.

I wish you would say to Sir Duncan McGregor [Inspector-General of the RIC] that it is much to be deprecated that Constables while dischg their duty in guarding a witness who has given his evidence on oath should <u>interrogate</u> that witness & endeavour to catch him in contradictions. It is not their business nor their duty. I lay no more regard to such talk than to the whistling of the wind. After a witness has been examined and cross-examined in open court and searched in every possible manner & thus Judge and jury are satisfied he is telling on his oath [the] truth & thus all the other circumstances of the case confirm his statement – it is arrant nonsense to seek to impeach the evidence on oath by such talk as the car boy and the constables detail. …[7]

TIPPERARY MP'S QUESTIONS

Two weeks later, on 18 June, The O'Donoghue opened his question in the House of Commons by stating 'that the greatest excitement prevailed in the county he represented on the subject of the question he was going to put in reference to the execution of the two Cormacks for the alleged murder of John Ellis'. He went on to state that the excitement had its origin in

no unworthy feeling of sympathy for the crime of murder, but from a general belief that the course adopted at the trial, and previous to the event, was contrary to the ordinary mode of judicial investigation in a free country and evinced on the part of the authorities rather a desire to punish someone than a determination to discriminate carefully between the innocent and the guilty (hear, hear).

He asked the Attorney-General to lay on the table of the House a copy of the notes taken by the Solicitor-General for Ireland in his examination of the carman and two policemen as well as 'the informer Burke', alongside a copy of Burke's evidence in the Cormack trial. He then gave a résumé of the case to the assembled MPs, the main thrust of which was to draw attention to the difference between Thomas Burke's evidence at the inquest and his evidence at the trial. He pointed out that Burke was a 'spontaneous and free witness' at the inquest but had been three months in gaol before the trial. He felt that if either of his accounts were true it was the one at the inquest. He referred to the alleged threat by Resident Magistrate Jones to Burke, that 'you will stay in gaol till you rot', and the effect it might have on the young Burke, which threat, he pointed out, 'Mr Jones did not contradict'.

Referring again to Burke's alleged confession to the car driver, The

O'Donoghue commented that 'it was a most extraordinary proceeding that Burke could be put out of the way so that those who wished to sift his statement could not do so'.

The MP for Tipperary then went on to claim that Judge Keogh 'charged the jury in a manner which he hoped would not often occur in this realm.' and that 'there were but few in the crowded courthouse who were not shocked at the demeanour of the judge, who laid aside the calm and impartial air which should characterise the bench to assume the excited tones of the impassioned advocate'. Newspaper reports of Keogh's charge to the jury do not convey that impression, but his tone and language in addressing the Cormacks directly after conviction was extreme, apparently sparked by their continued protestations of innocence.

The O'Donoghue was supported by Charles Gilpin, MP for Northhampton borough and a member of the Society of Friends, who was a campaigner against capital punishment. He believed that on this occasion 'the course taken by the Crown was contrary to the spirit of British law'.

John Bagwell also spoke, 'to bear his testimony to the fact', he said, 'that the excitement which prevailed in Tipperary on account of this trial was not at all exaggerated'.

The A-G Defends
Attorney-General Whiteside stood over the conduct of the investigation and the credibility of the key Crown witnesses. He dismissed the conversation that had taken place between Burke and the car driver on the way to Roscrea, saying, 'that neither of them was on his oath and anything that was said could not be allowed to impeach the testimony given on oath, sifted by cross-examination'. He said that had he himself been in Ireland he would not have recalled Burke from Liverpool (again a rebuke to the Solicitor-General, this time in public). He refused to disclose the whereabouts of Thomas Burke or Timothy Spillane. 'The Crown', he said, 'never deserted those whose lives might be placed in jeopardy by their telling the truth'.

Whiteside's reply, to say the least, was sparing with the facts, as he did not disclose that Constable Arthur's and sub-Constable Kenny's affidavits tallied independently with the car driver's story. He also ignored the 'in gaol till you rot' allegation. The resurrection of this subject in the Anne Brophy civil case (Chapter 15) was to show that the prosecution team led by Whiteside had at least attempted in the course of the Cormacks' trial to verify the allegation.

The matter was then dropped.[8]

The ethos of the forum to which the Irish MP was appealing is revealed in a paragraph in the *Cork Examiner* – from the pen of an insider, John

Francis Maguire, MP for Dungarvan, who was also the paper's proprietor and principal editor and doubled as the paper's London correspondent.

The O'Donoghue made an admirable statement ... whatever sympathy was excited by the statement was soon dissipated by the reply ... as the details of the assassination were described by the Attorney-General. It should be a very strong case, indeed, of misconduct on the part of the judge and jury, that could induce the House of Commons to interfere, where the victims were only a couple of Tipperary peasants, ... such is the profound horror in which the crime and its perpetrators are held in England ... I know scarcely anything of the case in question; I merely allude to the feeling which its recital evoked.[9]

Pursuing the Question

On 9 July The O'Donoghue tabled another question to Attorney-General Whiteside. This time he wanted to know whether 'the false character' of Burke's evidence at the trial, as revealed to the car driver, had 'been confirmed by Burke on his examination before the Solicitor-General for Ireland', and whether the Government intended to take steps to apprehend Burke.

Whiteside explained that Burke was examined, not by the Solicitor-General, but before a magistrate, and it was found that there was no reason to detain him.

A supplementary question by a Wexford MP, Patrick McMahon, said that the general impression was that Burke had repeated under examination that his evidence against the Cormacks was false. Was that true? All he wanted from Whiteside was a 'yes' or 'no'. The Attorney-General replied by reading the Solicitor-General's statement confirming the examination by the magistrate. He re-affirmed in the inviolability of a jury verdict:

It was very painful in a case of this kind that concerned the administration of justice that after a trial of two days, and after a witness had been examined by eminent counsel, and his testimony believed by a jury, it should be sought to impeach it by the simple uncorroborated statement of a man who was taking him to the seaboard.

As on the previous occasion he made no mention of the statements by Constables Arthur and Kenny which did corroborate that of Gleeson, the car driver.

Another supplementary by John F. Maguire elicited the information that Whiteside had not actually seen Burke's statement. 'The man was asked certain questions, he answered them, and was let go about his business'.

Eleven days later, 18 July, The O'Donoghue asked Whiteside 'whether it was the intention of the government to bring up Timothy Spillane as a witness on any future occasion?' The A-G replied that 'no criminal trial was at present pending in which it would be necessary to examine Spillane'. This was not correct, as the Patrick Maher case, on the calendar for the Nenagh summer assizes and for which Spillane was being detained as a Crown witness, was adjourned in July to the 1859 spring assizes.[10]

SPOTLIGHT ON SADLEIR AGAIN

During the course of his question on 18 June The O'Donoghue referred to an extraordinary incident that had occurred at Thurles petty sessions the previous week.[11] The O'Donoghue held that it and Burke's alleged confession justified a parliamentary investigation.

It involved John Sadleir, Thurles bridewell keeper, who had summoned John Walsh for allegedly calling him 'an Orange dog'. The case was dismissed and a second case was brought forward for hearing. In this Sadleir had brought a charge against John Walsh's brother, Cornelius, an employee of Matthew Quinlan, Stationer, Stamp Distributor and Clerk of the Petty Sessions. Apparently, when Sadleir had gone into Quinlan's shop to procure summonses against John Walsh, Cornelius Walsh advised him to drop the matter.

Cornelius also said to Sadleir that he ought to be ashamed to show his face in consequence of what he did, as 'it not only injured you but others like you in the town' – obviously referring to the unorthodox method employed by Sadleir to procure evidence against the Cormacks, and perhaps also referring to damage to the standing of local public officials like, say, his employer, Matthew Quinlan and/or to its effect on the Protestant community. Walsh's remark, as far as Sadleir was concerned, constituted 'threatening language'.

Walsh's solicitor, Daniel Molony, then produced a letter which Sadleir identified as in his handwriting. The solicitor then read it out to the court.

If Mr Dwyer [Edward Dwyer, who had been the Cormacks' solicitor] will have the goodness to oblige the writer of this with an interview he may hear something that will enable him to sift the truth or falsity of the statements made by Burke or Spillane against the unfortunate Cormacks. The writer of this would not wish to be seen going into your place and will therefore wait on the railway bridge until he sees you coming and will then proceed towards Anthony Dwyer's farm, where they may speak without being seen by any person. J.

Sadleir admitted it was written after the execution of the Cormacks. Challenged by Molony that the use of the term, 'unfortunate Cormacks', indicated that he had sympathy for them, he got excited and said he had no sympathy for them. Solicitor Molony said, 'then the letter is a lie', to which Sadleir replied, in a great state of excitement, 'it is a lie so far as I made use of Spillane and Burke's names ... because I knew it would have the effect of calling out Mr Dwyer'.

Solicitor Dwyer intervened to say he had met with Sadleir but he would not divulge ever what had passed between them. Sadleir said he had not got Resident Magistrate Jones's permission to write the letter. He caused a further sensation when he said, 'I cannot answer that', to Moloney's question, 'you now positively say that the letter was untrue, that it was a lie. Then there is nothing to be sifted about the evidence of Spillane and Burke?'

After some more exchanges between Sadleir and Moloney the magistrates took control, had the Clerk read out the letter again, ordered a copy to be made of it and then dismissed the case against Cornelius Walsh. The atmosphere was captured thus by one newspaper:

> Those Justices [of the Peace, i.e. magistrates] ... were thunderstruck: they had not a word to say; they looked at each other; they looked at Sadleir; they shook their heads; one of them rapped frequently with his fingers against the top framework of the bench, and still looked at Sadleir and looked at his brother Justices.[12]

3. THE NENAGH MEETING

Despite the rebuffs in parliament, the matter was not dropped on the home front and another effort was mounted to have the case enquired into. This culminated in the convening of a public meeting for Nenagh on Monday 30 August 1858. The names appended to the convening notice spanned the north and south ridings and included high profile personalities like Archbishop William Leahy, The O'Donoghue, MP, John Bagwell, MP, Frederick Lidwell, JP, William Hackett, JP, now Mayor of Clonmel, Alderman J Hackett, JP, John Lanigan, JP. The numerous clergy who signed included Rev. John Maher, C.C., Dunkerrin; Rev. John Kenyon, P.P., Templederry; Rev. Thomas O'Carroll, C.C., Clonoulty; Rev. John Scanlan, Adm., Nenagh; Rev. Dean Walter Cantwell, P.P. Cashel; Rev. Wm. Morris, P.P., Borrisoleigh; Rev. M. Power, Powerstown, Clonmel. The notice carried up to 3,500 signatures. The requisition with all the names appeared in four successive issues of the *LR & TV*. Solomon Lalor Cambie, JP, Killoran, Moyne, a signatory and who had been a grand juror at the spring assizes, chaired a sub-committee set up to agree proposed resolutions.[13]

The planned meeting caused some concern to the Chief Secretary, Lord Naas. He wrote to Under Secretary Larcom on 21 August suggesting that 'it would be wise to send a detective or two into Tipperary to gather some precise information as to the meeting at Nenagh. From what Bagwell and O'Donoghue told me in London ... the R.M.s ought to be told to send all the information they can get. ...' [14]

Monday's proceedings began at noon when a large party, accompanied by a band, marched out the Limerick road to meet and escort The O'Donoghue into Nenagh. Within an hour he had taken his place as chairman on a platform erected in front of the courthouse. From this position he could see a large black flag flying on the top of the keep of Nenagh castle, a hundred yards away, emblazoned with the words, well-known by now, 'in gaol till you rot'.

The function of the meeting was to have four agreed resolutions proposed, seconded and adopted in public. The thrust of the resolutions was similar to that of The O'Donoghue's question in the House of Commons in June – that a parliamentary investigation be conducted into all the circumstances of the trial and execution of the Cormack brothers. The language reflected the regard in which the embittered and articulate majority held both the ruling elite and the administration of the law.

The first resolution, proposed by Thomas Lalor Cambie, Templemore, made sweeping and generalised charges against the entire magistracy, grand jury and petty jurors of County Tipperary, as well as the judge in the case.

• That, as the taking away of human life is the highest responsibility assumed by human law, the English Constitution in committing the power of life or death to the judgement of a few individuals, has jealously provided every precaution, that in the words of a recognised authority, 'when the subject shall happen to be summoned to the decision of his fate by the fallible conscience of a few of his fellow-creatures, he may always find in them advocates and never adversaries':

• That a partisan Magistracy, witnesses of doubtful veracity, or proven sinister character, Grand Juries of long-cherished prejudices, Petit Juries of known hostility, are *each* and *all* antagonistic to the spirit and letter of said Constitution – and consequently must ever produce deep-rooted discontent, making of the court and its different forms a tribunal inspiring public distrust instead of public confidence:

• That such are notoriously the characteristic features which have frequently marked the administration of Justice in this country; aggravated lately by the still more unconstitutional anomaly of a Judge acting adversary to the accused – thus teaching the people to regard the law as its enemy, and not its protector.

The seconder, Rev. John Kenyon, P.P., Templederry, used stronger language still. Kenyon had played a leading role in the Young Ireland era in which he had won particular fame as a trenchant public speaker as well as a regular letter writer to the newspapers.[15]

Now at Nenagh in August, his speech treated of justice, truth, religious tolerance, and renewing 'their baptismal vows of patriotism in Tipperary'. It elicited 'loud cheers' and 'hear hears' but contributed nothing constructive to the resolution.

He said the first feeling which he experienced at finding himself one of a meeting of Tipperarymen assembled to petition the British parliament for a fragment of justice in a flagrant case of injustice, was one of shame ...Time was in Ireland when the priests of Ireland – aye, and the bishops, too – would scorn to petition the Saxon parliament ... They would give justice to their own people, but you are a people foreign to them; they have their heels upon your necks, and their hands in your pockets, and they have no notion of recognising you as their equals, or of dispensing to you impartial justice.

KENYON ON KEOGH
He showed a particular vindictiveness towards Judge Keogh, which would appear to have political origins dating back to Keogh's defection from the Irish party in 1852. It was vintage Kenyon who now grouped 'the ape, the monkey and the unjust judge' as 'the meanest, the vilest, the lowest of creation'.

And such an unjust judge, and such a vile man was that Keogh, a man who, for his deadly treason to his country, if true justice was administered to him – not the caricature, the mockery of justice he dispensed in yonder courthouse – he would, years since have hung upon a gallows fifty feet high (cheers and laughter). He was one of those who traded upon the credulity of the men of Ireland. They had been too long duped, and he was one of those who, pretending to be their friend, stabbed them in the heart. They should petition parliament to hang him (cheers and laughter).

One wonders if Kenyon's vitriol, which was carried in the local and national papers, started the revilement of Keogh and the apportioning of major blame to him for the execution of the Cormacks, manifested later on the occasion of the exhumation and reburial and in ballads. The same tone is evident on one of the plaques erected at the Cormack mausoleum in Loughmore.

SECTARIANISM PERCEIVED
Rev. Michael Scanlan, P.P., Cloughjordan, proposed the second resolution which was aimed specifically at a perceived sectarian bias in the selection of petit/petty juries to serve at the assizes and, accordingly, to seek to have

the method of selection abolished.

• That the Assizes Petit Jury panel of this county has always been regarded by the vast majority of its inhabitants as a glaring outrage on our administrative Criminal Justice:- that at this moment the first fifty or sixty names on that Panel include the names of some *five or six Catholics only*, and these usually non-attending Jurors – that the foremost and available Jurors, therefore, empanelled to try the unfortunate Catholic accused must be, almost to a man, taken from the ranks of a party who have ever manifested the most open and avowed hostility to his class, his religion, and his rights, thereby converting his right of challenge of the accused into a mockery, and his trial by a Jury of his fellow-countrymen into a mere delusion and a snare.

Vigorous complaints about a disproportionate representation of the majority religion were not new in 1858. Earlier in the year the *Limerick Reporter & Tipperary Vindicator* had alleged that 'for the last fourteen years petty juries at assizes are not constituted with a fair proportion of Catholics .... The lists from which the jurors are selected contain an overwhelming preponderance of Catholics ... nearly ten to one, but what do we see here year after year. ...

The *LR & TV* alleged that merchants and shopkeepers, eligible by law, were not called upon in North Tipperary, although they were in Limerick. 'In what is renting of some acres of land higher than the business of the trader?'

The *LR & TV* attack arose from a head count they had done for the most recent quarter sessions at Nenagh. It drew a response from Gerald Fitzgerald, under-sheriff for Co. Tipperary: 'I should greatly regret to exclude any person qualified, solely on his religion ... not acquainted with the religious belief of ten of the forty gentlemen summoned to attend.'[16]

Alderman William Hackett, Mayor of Clonmel, the seconder of Scanlan's resolution, enlarged a bit on its sentiments. His observation that 'the whole of Tipperary was this day represented by [only] one man', was a barb aimed at the county's other member of parliament who had not come to the meeting, Laurence Waldron, as well as the MPs for Clonmel and Cashel, John Bagwell and Sir Timothy O'Brien respectively, likewise absent.

THE CROWN WITNESSES
The third resolution, proposed by Rev. Daniel Lanigan, P.P., Kilcommon, was more focused – directed at the questionable character of the Crown witnesses and the quality of their evidence in the Cormack trial, and on the government's failure to respond positively to the demand for an inquiry.

• That the evils we complain of have had their unhappy consummation in the case of the ill-fated Brothers Cormack; that the jury in that case was not fairly chosen; that the witnesses were not of reliable veracity, the one being an accomplice [Spillane], the other an acknowledged perjurer, and an accomplice likewise [Burke], and the third, a jailer [Sadleir], whose more than doubtful testimony, as to what he said he overheard in the prison, was improperly and unconstitutionally admitted in evidence; that the acknowledgement made by the principal witness in this case – namely, 'that he had been threatened to be left to rot in gaol if he refused to give evidence'; and his subsequent confession, attested by the affidavits of three respectable witnesses, are acts loudly calling for the strictest investigation; and that we cannot let this opportunity pass without recording, thus publicly, our utter disappointment at the miserable evasion whereby the government have sought to justify their refusal of such investigation.

George Burke, solicitor, Liscahill, Thurles, in seconding the resolution, raised the question of the reliability of Thomas Burke's evidence because of Resident Magistrate Jones's alleged threat. If untrue, Jones, he believed, should have come forward and said so, thus proving Burke unreliable. George Burke also made an interesting point about the first petty jury (who failed to agree a verdict in William Cormack's trial) to the effect that some of them did not believe Thomas Burke, thus recapitulating on a point in the Archbishop Leahy memorial to the Lord Lieutenant.

FOCUS ON KEOGH AGAIN
The final resolution was proposed by Rev. John Scanlan, P.P., Nenagh. This laid the blame for the conviction of the Cormacks fair and square on the shoulders of Judge Keogh.

• That it is the especial duty of the State to require from the judgement seat impartial and unsuspected justice, while to the people it belongs to complain, if the caprice of the Judge will over-rule their chartered rights; or, if in his interest, or his anger, their lives are endangered; that in the opinion of this meeting the conviction of the Cormacks was not according to justice – that their lives were wrongfully taken away – and that in their case Mr Judge Keogh is fairly suspected of having outraged the decorum of the court and trifled with the spirit of the Constitution; and that it becomes a solemn duty to petition the legislature for a serious and searching inquiry into the part that learned functionary has taken in this remarkable trial.

In his explanatory speech after reading the resolution Fr Scanlan said Keogh's pronouncement that Thomas Burke was not an accomplice enabled the Crown to present him as a credible witness. This credibility was endorsed by the judge's direction to the jury that Burke's failure at the inquest to identify William Cormack as the man who fired the shot was because of fear of William – thus clearing him of a perjury charge.

Fr Scanlan also referred to the matter of Counsellor Johnstone's objection on behalf of the Cormacks to the judge's charge to the jury that Burke was not an accomplice and his request that the jury be recalled so that Johnstone could explain to them what, in the eyes of the law, constituted an informer and then they could come to whatever conclusion themselves. This was done but, according to Fr Scanlan, before the jury retired again Keogh said that 'it would be an absurdity to look upon Burke as an accomplice'. This, Fr Scanlan held, was not the act of an impartial judge.

That quoted contribution by Keogh does not appear in the *Limerick Reporter & Tipperary Vindicator* account of the legal exchanges at the trial. With hindsight it is a wonder that Fr Scanlan did not see to it that that point was made in the Cormacks' memorial to the Lord Lieutenant which he witnesssed.

The resolution was seconded by Thomas Parker O'Flanagan, Killenaule in South Tipperary.[17]

In the Eyes of the Beholders

A spate of newspaper coverage, which lasted right through to the end of September, followed the Nenagh meeting. But, firstly, a look at how it was seen by official eyes in Nenagh gaol and Thurles respectively.

To J.G. Jones

I hasten to send you a few particulars of the Meeting just concluded (1/2 past 4 o'clock p.m.). The number of persons present was very small, not exceeding on the most liberal calculation 700 persons, and those nearly altogether of the lower classes. But one M.P. was present, The O'Donoghue, the rest expected wisely stayed away from various excuses.

The drift of the whole proceeding turned out to be nearly what I prepared you for in my note of yesterday, as Judge Keogh's conduct was made altogether the topic of the speakers, and you were alluded to but in connexion with that saying of Bourke's 'You may stop in Gaol until you rot' which was introduced by Bourke the Attorney, and you were blamed for not refuting it at once, as they believed it to be a falsehood. On the whole you escaped their attacks I may say altogether – As for this place, you can fancy how little excitement there was about it, when I myself was out part of the time listening to them.

I expect this meeting will prove a damper and that things will soon settle down again, and that as soon as public opinion will take its just course – you need care little or any one connected with it, for their projected investigation.

Thos Rock

[To] Col. Larcom.

I send you a note I received by this post from Mr Rock, the Governor of Nenagh Prison by which you will perceive that the great County Meeting, so long anticipated by the dissatisfied, was, as I conjectured, a perfect failure, as I can learn – it was composed of priests in <u>abundance</u>, needy Attornies & the rabble of Nenagh; the greatest exertions had been used to induce the Farmers to attend, but they prudently remained at home.

I hope after this disappointment we shall now be permitted to remain quiet. John Gore Jones.[18]

The meeting was reported, or commented on later, in national newspapers, the *Freeman's Journal, Globe, Daily Express, Daily Mail, Morning Star, Dublin Evening Post* and the *Belfast Mercury*, as well as the local *Limerick Reporter & Tipperary Vindicator* and the *Nenagh Guardian.*[19] A newspaper's political allegiance – unionist or nationalist – determined whether the comment was for or against the sentiments voiced in the resolutions.

For example: '… not more than four thousand, consisting of men, women – described elsewhere in the paper as 'the weaker sex' – and children, out of a population of 340,000 people, could be influenced or coerced to attend …' wrote the *Nenagh Guardian*, a consistent supporter of the establishment, while the nationalist *Freeman's Journal* stated 'there were eight to ten thousand persons present and a very strong feeling seemed to prevail among the people on the subject'. One notes that both figures are several times the estimate conveyed to RM Jones by that loyal servant, Thomas Rock.

The pro-government papers honed in on Fr Kenyon's speech. One suggested he should be sued for slandering the judge who could not defend himself. They also raised the question of why an appeal wasn't lodged because of the purported irregularities in the appointment of the jury and the mis-directment by the judge. They said the judge had deliberately given the prisoners the 'long day' – the time span between sentence and date of execution, usually only two to three weeks but in the Cormacks' case over seven weeks.

As the era had a high consciousness of sectarian divisions, it was pointed out that Keogh, Fitzgerald who had been Whiteside's predecessor as Attorney-General, one of the RMs, some of the grand jury and petty jury, were of all of the same faith as the Cormacks – Roman Catholics.

The pro-Cormacks press gave summaries of the trial, referred to the Burke 'confession' to the car driver, and voiced criticism of the administration of justice and of the officials involved at local and national level. Edward Dwyer, Thurles, the Cormacks' solicitor, reacted strongly to the *Daily Mail's* suggestion that there must have been a confession from the Cormacks and that those engaged in their defence were keeping quiet about it.

113

... I was their attorney and in justice to their memories, and my own character I feel bound to give the whole statement the most unqualified contradiction. It is not only wholly untrue – but it happens to be the reverse of the truth – for not only did these poor men not confess their guilt to me, but they at all times, before and after their conviction gave the most pathetic and solemn assurance of their innocence, not merely of the murder of Mr Ellis but of any participation whatsoever in it directly or indirectly ... So far, therefore, from there being, as you allege, no doubt of 'the justice of their punishment' there is a general well-founded belief – in which I most fully share – that their execution was a lamentable miscarriage of justice.

It is right to say that the counsel who defended the Cormacks had not any personal communication with them, and therefore, could not well have received any such confession, as you refer to, from them. ...[20]

NOTES

1 *NG*, 15 & 29 May 1858.
2 *NG*, 2 June 1858.
3 NA, CSORP 1858, No. 14921: Trant to Larcom 17 June 1858.
4 *NG*, 14 Mar 1857. An advocate of Tenant Right and formally described as Independent Opposition, The O'Donoghue (Daniel O'Donoghue) secured a majority of 920 over Laurence Waldron, a Liberal, Killenaule & Dublin. The seat became vacant when James Sadleir, MP, was expelled from the House of Commons on the collapse of the Tipperary Joint Stock Bank of which he was Managing Director. The villain in the collapse was his brother John, MP for Carlow, and friend of Judge William Keogh. John Sadleir and Keogh as MPs had incurred widespread wrath when they defected from the Independent Irish Party after the 1852 general election to take positions in the coalition government. The O'Donoghue and Waldron were returned unopposed for the county's two seats in the 1857 General Election.
5 NLI, Larcom Papers MS 7636; copy in Cormack file, Co Library, Thurles.
6 *Hansard, H.C.*, Vol. CL, pp. 1311-12, 1 June 1858.
7 NLI, Larcom Papers MS 7636.
8 *Hansard, H.C.,* Vol. CLI, pp. 16-26, 18 June 1858; *NG*, 23 June 1858.
9 *LR & TV*, 22 June 1858 quoted the *Cork Examiner.*
10 *Hansard, H.C.,* Vol CLI, pp 1194 & 1785, 9 & 18 July 1858; *NG*, 20 July 1858.
11 *LR & TV*, 15 June 1858.
12 ditto.
13 *LR & TV*, 20, 24, 27, 31 August 1858.
14 NLI, Larcom Papers MS 7636: Under Secretary Larcom from Lord Naas, 21 Aug 1858; copy in Cormack file, Co Library, Thurles.
15 Donal A. Murphy, 'John Kenyon, National Figure and Templederry's P.P.' in *Templederry My Home* (1980), pp. 18-25; Ignatius Murphy, *The Diocese of Killaoe 1800-1850* and *The Diocese of Killaoe 1850-1904* (Dublin 1992, 1995), have multiple references throughout each volume. Kenyon had caused a furore in his native Limerick during an election by his denunciation of Daniel O'Connell immediately after the Liberator's death abroad in 1847. A decade later, in January 1858, he again intervened in a Limerick parliamentary election with an extensive advertisement in the local newspaper and an aggressive attempt to speak out of turn at the election itself.
16 *LR & TV*, 15 Jan 1858.
17 *FJ*, 31 Aug 1858; *NG*, 1 Sept 1858.
18 NLI, Larcom Papers MS No.7636; copy in the Cormack file, Co. Library, Thurles.
19 *Freeman's Journal*, 31 Aug; *Daily Express*, 31 Aug; *NG*, 1 & 4 Sept; *Globe*, 1 Sept; *Morning Star*, 3 Sept; *LR & TV*, 3 Sept; *Daily Mail*, 6 Sept; *DEP*, 9 Sept; *Belfast Mercury*, 10 Sept 1858.
20 *Evening Mail*, 1 Sept 1858.

Chapter 15

Patrick Maher and Anne Brophy

Timothy Spillane's statement in December 1857 that the gun used to kill John Ellis belonged to a Patrick Maher of Brittas, Thurles, led to Maher being suspected as 'the party who was fitting up a conspiracy to shoot Colonel Knox, Brittas Castle'. Maher was duly detained for examination.[1] This information is contained in a letter written by George Goold, RM, Thurles, to Under Secretary Larcom in early January 1858. The case was complicated by the fact that Maher had retained a solicitor who was now 'requiring us to commit him [for trial] and stating that in the event of non-compliance he is instructed to move for a *Habeas Corpus* [a common law writ to a gaoler to produce a prisoner in person to a court and to state the reasons for detention]. This I take as mere nonsense … .'

Goold's main purpose in writing seems to have been to get assurance that any expense incurred in relation to this would be recouped. Accordingly, he was urging that a direction be sought from the Attorney-General. Indeed, he expressed a wish to meet with the A-G on the matter as 'much more could be done in a half hour's conversation than by several letters'.

Maher's trial was down for hearing at the 1858 Tipperary North Riding spring assizes – the one at which the Cormacks were tried. As already mentioned, Timothy Spillane was to appear as a witness for the Crown in the case. The prosecution sought and was granted a postponement.

At the summer assizes in July Mr George, QC, applied for another postponement, based on information from RM Jones that the principal witness, Michael Mockler, had absconded, having received, Jones claimed, 'a large sum of money' from Maher. Affidavits by Maher and his mother, countering this claim, were produced. Mrs Maher further claimed that, though she had informed Jones of Mockler's whereabouts, no attempt had been made to arrest him. Charles Rolleston, Maher's defence counsel, held that Knox's evidence would suffice for the case to be heard. This was disputed and the trial postponed. Rolleston made a great plea for bail but this was refused.[2]

By the spring assizes of 1859 Maher had been in gaol for sixteen months. However, notwithstanding the expense incurred in keeping him and Timothy Spillane in custody, the court was told, without explanation, that there would be no trial and Maher was discharged by proclamation.[3]

ANNE BROPHY

There was an even more extraordinary case of an incidental victim of the Ellis murder investigation. She was twelve-year-old Anne Brophy, Kilrush, daughter of one of John Trant's ploughmen. At the instigation of RM Jones she was brought to Thurles bridewell on 28 October 1857 – the police later held that she came willingly and was not under arrest. Anne worked on occasions for John Ellis. The reason for her detention and for the cruel treatment meted out to her during that period, emerged when civil proceedings for her false imprisonment were taken by her father against Jones.

The case was heard in the Court of the Exchequer, Dublin, in October 1858 before the Lord Chief Baron, Rt Hon. David Richard Pigot, and a special jury.[4] Nine witnesses were sworn and examined and five Queen's Counsel were in action. Its connection with the Cormacks' case ensured high media coverage.

This court hearing, more than that of the Cormacks, conveys the helplessness of a person under detention/arrest – without legal representation or contact with family. It reveals the powers enjoyed by RMs and the extent to which the two based in Co. Tipperary were prepared to go to pressurise an innocent person in pursuance of their investigation.

Like the Cormacks's names, Anne Brophy's is noticeably absent from the RMs' correspondence with Dublin Castle.

RM JONES IN THE DOCK

As Jones did not give evidence in the Cormack trial, the account of his handling of the Ellis murder investigation, which unfolded in his evidence at this hearing, is of interest. From it we learn that Ellis had enjoyed the constant protection of two policemen for up to about a year before the murder, but that the RM had never given instructions to the police to patrol the roads on nights when Ellis was returning home. However, he learnt at the inquest on Ellis that the Dovea police were in the habit of doing so, but did not on the night of the murder, 22 October 1857. On enquiring their reason for this Jones was told that information had come into the barrack that evening that Ellis would not be coming home that night. Jones said that 'he was led to suppose that the information had come from Anne Brophy'.

He then gave instructions to Head Constable Barry, to have her brought in for examination. Jones emphasised that she was not arrested. Eliza (Lizzie) Douglas, daughter of sub-Constable Douglas, whom Anne Brophy had allegedly told that Ellis would not be coming home, was also brought in.

The girls were then questioned separately by Jones in the presence of fellow RM, George Goold.

Anne Brophy admitted, on oath according to Jones, that on the evening of 22 October she had told Lizzie Douglas that Ellis would not be coming home that night. Jones, understandably, formed the impression that this piece of information 'was the very key to the inquiry and, acting as magistrate, considered it my bounden duty to obtain any information connected with the statement ...'

On further questioning, Anne Brophy revealed to him that she had heard persons talking in the Ellis yard about Ellis not coming home that night. She mentioned William Cormack and a Denis Cullagh, but went mute when asked to name the other person. Jones was emphatic that she never said she did not know it.

Jones then focused on getting the name of that third person. This led to her being detained for further examinations. Jones went on:

I never suggested to her the name Cormack, I had no earthly motive of the kind, most unquestionably my object in asking those questions was not to hunt up evidence against the Cormacks; on the contrary when she named William Cormack we told her that her statement was not true ...

The latter remark appears to shows that it was known at that early stage of the investigation that William Cormack had gone to Templemore on the morning of 22 October for a load of coal for Mrs Ellis.

Jones then recounted how a committal order was signed and Anne Brophy was detained in Thurles bridewell. She was subjected to weekly examination by him in the presence of RM Goold – usually in the bridewell keeper's room but once in Thurles courthouse. She was also sent to the county gaol in Nenagh for examination. The purpose of all this questioning was to get her to reveal the name of the (third) person in the yard.

Under cross-examination Jones denied that he intended her to be a Crown witness, saying, 'I did not keep her as a Crown witness but because she would not fulfill the law and give evidence ...' He also said that he had 'nothing more to do with making a Crown witness than to recommend him'. He admitted that while in detention 'there was an understanding' that Anne Brophy was not to be allowed to communicate with anyone, even her parents.

IN GAOL TILL YOU ROT
Counsellor Lynch for Anne Brophy now availed of the opportunity to elicit from Jones, under oath, the facts of the threat which Thomas Burke alleged Jones had made to him.

Jones: I heard Burke swear at the trial that I said he would rot in gaol if he did not give evidence against the Cormacks; that statement was false. I knew that the credibility of Burke was one of the turning points in the case. Mr Carmichael [Clerk of the Crown for Tipperary North Riding] said to me at the moment 'they' (meaning the Crown counsel) 'want to know if that is true'. I replied 'no, certainly not; it is not true'. After that I did not communicate to the Attorney-General the falsehood of that witness, I conceived he had heard it from Mr Carmichael. I did not communicate the falsehood of that statement to the prisoners' counsel. I was not asked.

Lynch, QC: Did you know that Burke was the only corroborative evidence of Spillane the approver?

Jones: There was a great many other corroborative circumstances. I have had great experience as a magistrate and I never met a clearer case.

In his evidence George Goold, RM, confirmed Jones's account of how the questioning was conducted and that the girl had been sworn before each session commenced.

Sub-Constable William Douglas confirmed that the reason the police did not patrol the roads on the night of 22 October was because his daughter told him Ellis would not be coming home.[5] He had ascertained from her that Anne Brophy had told her this. Under cross-examination by Charles Rolleston, QC, acting for Anne Brophy, Douglas said he was aware that the car had gone to Templemore railway station to collect Ellis but he then withdrew this statement saying that it was a mistake. Patrolling the roads, he explained, was done on an irregular basis on instructions from the Head Constable.

GAOL TREATMENT

Prior to all the above evidence Anne Brophy, under examination in court, had given her account of the conditions under which she had been detained and the interrogation she had been subjected to. The fact that she admitted she had lied to Jones put a question mark over her credibility. But her account of the conditions and the interrogation sessions were confirmed in the evidence of George Goold, RM, and John Sadleir, the Thurles bridewell keeper.

She recalled the details of her 'arrest' by policeman Douglas who took her to the 'jail house' in Thurles where she encountered John Gore Jones, George Goold and Head Constable Barry. She denied that she was put on oath by Jones. She recounted that in answer to a question put by Jones she admitted that she had told the Douglas girl that Ellis would not be coming home that night, but denied to him that she had heard this from anyone in the yard. She said after this session of questions she was taken to a small room with a bed, and locked in. She was kept there for a week, being let out every morning to 'the backyard inside the jail. ... The weather was cold and there was no fire in the cell ... I did not see my mother or father during that week.

After a week she was brought before the above three gentlemen again and questioned by Jones along the same lines as before. She said she could tell them no more. She was locked up again by John Sadleir under the same conditions. A fortnight passed, she said, before she was brought out to Thurles courthouse where she was subjected to the same line of questioning as before, but this time by both Jones and Goold. She saw her father on the street on her way to the courthouse but the 'peelers' would not allow him to speak to her. She denied being put on oath prior to questioning. She was returned to the cell and kept there for some days.

She was awoken by John Sadleir at four o'clock in the morning and taken to Nenagh gaol by 'two peelers in a covered car' where she was detained for a 'fortnight and three days. Mr Rock, the governor of the jail examined me, I did not refuse to give evidence'. An objection by Mr Fitzgibbon, QC, to her recounting what went on in Nenagh, was sustained.

After two weeks in Nenagh Anne Brophy was taken back to Thurles, put in a cell without a fire and held for a further week. After that John Sadleir came and took her bed away, so she 'began to cry and roar and bawl and I was taken down and let out'. She said she was held for two months in all, during which time she saw no friends or family.

In cross-examination Counsellor Fitzgibbon elicited from her that it was about 7 o'clock that she told the Douglas girl that Ellis was not coming home. Then she turned her case upside down by stating that she heard Thomas Burke say that Ellis was not coming home, then saying that he did not say that but said he had taken Ellis to Templemore station the previous night; that she never heard anyone in the yard discussing whether he would be home or not and that what she told Resident Magistrate Jones was a lie. She enlarged on this under examination, saying that it was a lie to say Denny Cullagh was in the yard. Neither was William Cormack. Quizzed as to why she told lies to Jones she said she did not know. When Mr Fitzgibbon asked her to explain to the jury why she told Lizzie Douglas what she did, she said she did not know.

John Sadleir said in his evidence that he was complying with Resident Magistrate Jones's instructions in his treatment of Anne Brophy during her detention in the bridewell.

One must note that the era was within living memory of the introduction in 1833 of a 48-hour weekly working limit in their first year of work for children under eleven years of age[6]; thirty years ahead of a statutory provision that a parent was to attend an examination by a magistrate of a child under twelve[7]; almost thirty also ahead of a magistrate being enabled to take the evidence of children too young to understand the nature of an oath[8]; and fifty years ahead of major legislation for the protection of children[9].

For the duration of her detention in Thurles this child was virtually a non-person. The lack of humanity was aggravated by an absence of legality. An 1856 statute had spelled out that 'no magistrate shall have authority ... to interefere with the discipline of the prison'.[10]

THE CASE OF THE CORMACKS RAISED AGAIN

From the beginning it was clear that Anne Brophy's leading counsel, Charles Rolleston, was out to ensure that this case renewed the high profile of the Ellis murder and the trial and execution of Daniel and William Cormack. In his outline of the plaintiff's case to the jury he set about discrediting Jones on a few fronts. He focused firstly on Jones's conduct of the Ellis murder investigation, saying:

His duty in such a case was to endeavour to ascertain the truth, it was his duty to elicit evidence which would acquit the innocent as would convict the guilty. But from the commencement Mr Jones seemed to forget that such was his duty.

He then suggested that the story of John Ellis's alleged seduction of the Cormacks' sister was probably one of the reasons that Mr Jones believed them to be the perpetrators of the crime. He claimed immense dissatisfaction still existed at the manner in which the evidence was worked up against them. He said that Jones's threat to Burke was to force him to support Spillane's evidence, and his pressurising of Anne Brophy was to get her to admit that it was one of the Cormacks who said Ellis would not be home.

He quoted an 1851 statute which authorised a magistrate to commit a witness for eight days who refused to take an oath or, having taken it, refused to answer questions. That same legal provision did indeed allow a magistrate to 'adjourn the proceedings and commit the witness for the like period [eight days], and so again from time to time until he shall consent to be sworn or to testify as aforesaid'.[11] But Rolleston claimed that Anne Brophy did answer and that Jones grossly overstretched the law by holding the twelve-year-old 'in solitary confinement for sixty days'.

In his cross-examination of John Sadleir he asked him bluntly, 'Did you give evidence against the Cormacks?' Sadleir replied, 'Yes, I did'. Rolleston then elicited from him that he had told Mr Jones what he had heard in the eavesdropping session. He then challenged: 'you heard the information as governor of the gaol?', to which Sadleir replied, 'yes, in the discharge of my duty'. 'On your oath', said Rolleston, 'is it part of your duty to listen to conversation between criminals?' 'No', replied Sadleir. The bridewell keeper then explained that he was not aware at the time he told of the conversations that he could be produced as a witness.

CALL JAMES CARMICHAEL

Rolleston continued his questioning of Sadleir in the same vein until Counsellor Fitzgibbon objected. However, the presiding judge allowed it as it was 'directed to test the credit of the witness'. Rolleston also elicited from Sadleir that Anne Brophy had been sent to Nenagh 'to separate her from the Cormacks'.

Rolleston now caused some sensation by announcing that he proposed to call James Carmichael, Clerk of the Crown, to put a question to him about John Gore Jones's disclosure that the Crown counsel had wanted to know if the 'in gaol till you rot' allegation by Thomas Burke was correct. Rolleston's purpose was to establish if the statement made earlier by Jones was true. Mr Fitzgibbon objected and the Chief Baron ruled that the question could not be put.

Rolleston persisted, saying it was a very serious matter involving a public officer and that he was going to put the question to Carmichael anyway and the other side could then object.

James Carmichael was duly sworn. Rolleston put two questions to him on the subject but immediate objections by Mr Fitzgibbon prevented replies. Rolleston had succeeded in exposing another questionable aspect of Jones's conduct, one which had the potential of influencing the jury in favour of his present client.

It remains unanswered as to whether Carmichael did act as intermediary between the Crown counsel and Jones, and if so whether he conveyed to the Crown counsel the denial which Jones claimed he made.

Counsellors Lynch (for Brophy) and Armstrong (for Jones) in their addresses to the jury focused on the subject of the trial – whether or not Anne Brophy had endured unlawful arrest at the hands of Mr Jones and what damages she might be awarded.

Lynch made his plea on the grounds that the law, which only allowed detention of a witness for eight days, had been flaunted. He called on the jury to give Anne Brophy compensation for 'this outrage'.

Armstrong held that no instruction to arrest was given. He alleged the case was brought 'not to compensate Anne Brophy, but for the purpose of stabbing at the respect of the defendant and to try again the guilt of the Cormacks'.

JUDGEMENT

The Chief Baron in his charge to the jury ruled that the imprisonment had been illegal, and that the defendant had not adopted the course which the statute required. Anne Brophy's admission that she had told lies to Jones was now brought into the reckoning. If Jones, he said, had endeavoured to coerce Anne Brophy to 'give evidence she was not able to give, or if through ignorance or stupidity she really was incapable of giving any answers to the questions put to her, the defence had failed and the defendant was guilty of not only a violation of his duty but of a malicious act of imprisonment'. However, if the jury considered that the plaintiff withheld her answers to defeat public justice and was capable of giving the required information, he could not name any sum which would be low enough as compensation.

The jury, after an absence of an hour, found that Anne Brophy had been falsely imprisoned but awarded her the minimum damages of 6d. Their verdict showed that the Chief Baron's charge in relation to potential compensation had influenced them more than Counsellor Lynch's plea, 'that Anne Brophy had her early years marked with a prison sentence more severe than she would have been subjected to if convicted of a criminal offence', or his call on them to give her such damages as would compensate her 'for the loss of character and imminent danger to morals which this imprisonment was calculated to lead to'.[12]

'IF ONLY …'

Alluding to the incident in which Jones said that Carmichael, Clerk of the Crown, at the behest of the Crown counsel, had asked him if Burke's allegation was true and Jones's assumption that his denial had been communicated to them, the Chief Baron then recounted an anecdote from his own days on the assizes circuit.

A man was on trial, and a person intimated to the Crown counsel that there was a certain fact going to exculpate the prisoner; the fact was elicited, the prisoner was acquitted and he (the Chief Baron) upon the part of the Crown subsequently prosecuted the witness in the box for an attempt to bring about, by false testimony, the conviction of an innocent man.[13]

Without Carmichael's confirmation of Jones's statement the possibility remains that Thomas Burke's allegation of the 'rot in gaol' threat was true. However, it is unlikely that an officer of the law, Jones, would perjure himself in the circumstances. If Burke's claim were false his identification of the Cormacks as the murderers is brought into question. This brings his confession to the car driver and constables into the realm of truth and makes greed for the reward, rather than fear, the governing factor for his behaviour.

The Chief Baron's anecdote seems to imply, firstly, that he believed that Jones's denial had indeed been conveyed to the prosecution and, secondly, upon that presumption that the prosecuting/Crown counsel should have discounted Burke as a witness and facilitated discharge of the Cormacks. A failure of the prosecution led by Attorney-General Whiteside to inform the court of this undermining of Burke's credibility might account for Whiteside dodging the question in his House of Commons reply, even though The O'Donoghue specifically quoted the threat and said it had never been denied by the RM.

The final phase in 'the case of the Cormacks' was to be the presentation of the petition for a Parliamentary Inquiry. The only trace of this process which can be found is a report that the Committee were active in November finalising it. The *LR & TV* were confident that the Inquiry would 'reveal all'. Presumably the petition is amongst the 6,101 public petitions presented in 1859. Of these 689 were printed and of these committee reports emanated on 31.[14]

EXIT SADLEIR AND JONES

John Sadleir's career as bridewell keeper came to an end in 1858. He was the subject of a report to Dublin Castle in December of that year for 'alleged drunkenness'. He is described as the 'late bridewell keeper, Thurles', in official correspondence during the last six months of 1860.[15] A presentment or estimate was passed at the Tipperary North Riding summer assizes of 1873 for the sum of £16 13s 4d for his half-year's superannuation. The same amount was passed in 1898 – which suggests he was quite a young man in 1858.[16] The normal public servant works for forty years and enjoys a pension for, say, a further ten or fifteen: Sadleir did the reverse.

RM John Gore Jones lived an even more exciting life in the aftermath of the stirring events of 1857-8, at one point veering on the edge of Ellis's fate. In early March 1863 an attempt was made on his life as he travelled on horseback from Thurles to the petty sessions in Borrisoleigh. The attack occurred sometime after 10 a.m. on the main Thurles road where a boreen to the right leads to Lissaroon bog. A shot was fired from the ditch at the junction of the road and boreen and perforated Jones's coat. He suffered no injury and chased the two men. He saw them in a field alongside the boreen and later identified one of them as Philip Hayes, who worked for Andrew Ryan, Gortkelly, Borrisoleigh.

Hayes was tried at the July 1863 assizes in Nenagh. From evidence given at the trial it appears he was contracted by a Patrick Grady to accompany him to do the shooting. The jury was discharged after they failed to reach a verdict. Hayes was refused bail.[17]

The case came up for hearing again at the 1864 spring assizes. Hayes was found guilty and sentenced to 20 years penal servitude. Jones's connection with the conviction of the Cormacks was not mentioned as a motive for the attack.[18]

John Gore Jones had been commissioned as an RM in 1831. He died in Templemore in 1879 aged 82 years. He is buried in the Church of Ireland graveyard there, where his daughter, Helen Arabella, who died of tuberculosis in 1875, aged 25 years, is also interred.[19]

NOTES
1   NLI, Larcom Papers MS 7636.
2   *NG*, 20 July, 1858.
3   *NG*, 19 Mar 1859.
4   Murphy, *Two Tipperarys*, pp. 84, 92n. Pigot had some acquaintance with Tipperary, having been more or less imposed on Clonmel Borough as its MP in 1839, consequent on his appointment as Solicitor-General for Ireland. As a King's Counsel he had appeared before the Privy Council in 1837 for the Nenagh lobby in favour of the division of Co. Tipperary.
5   *FJ*, 27 Oct 1858. Lizzie and Maria Douglas worked with Ellis – Lizzie as a casual worker in the yard and Maria as a house servant. There is mention of Anne Brophy 'teasing hair' for a man making a horse collar, so she probably worked in the yard.
6   David Thomson, *England in the Nineteenth Century*, (London 1971), p. 47.
7   Criminal Law and Procedure (Ir) Act, 1887 (50 & 51 Vic., c. 20), s. 1(3).
8   Criminal Law Amendment Act, 1885 (48 & 49 Vic., c. 69), referenced by Anon in *Encyclopedia Britannica*, vol. 23, p. 440b, in relation to Benjamin Waugh, the English social reformer who founded the London Society for the Prevention of Cruelty to Children and assembled information which led to the passage of that act.
9   Children Act, 1908 (8 Edw. VII, c. 67).
10 Prisons (Ir) Act, 1856 (19 & 20 Vic., c. 68), s.4.
11 Petty Sessions (Ir) Act, 1851 (14 & 15 Vic., c. 93).
12 *FJ*, 27 Oct 1858, *NG*, 30 Oct 1858. Both the *NG* and *FJ* of 30 Oct carried lengthy editiorials critical of the conduct of the police on the night Ellis was murdered. They described their inaction as a result of listening 'to the gossip of two young girls', as 'a flagrant breach of duty'.
13 *FJ*, 27 Oct 1858.
14 LR & TV, 9 & 12 Nov 1858; NLI, PP Accounts & Papers, vol. L, 1861, p. 098.
15 NA, CSORP1858, 1860, No.s 2024, 15934.
16 *North Riding of the County of Tipperary , An Abstract of the presentments Passed by the Grand Jury*, Summer Assizes, 1 July 1873, p. 2; ditto, 1898, p. 1. We do not know if he continued living in Co. Tipperary. No death record was found for him

in Tipperary North, nor is he in the 1901 census for that riding.

17   *NG*, 27 July 1863.
18   *NG*, 23 Mar 1864. Hayes would serve his sentence in Mountjoy or Spike Island prisons. Transportation had been discontinued in 1856. Penal servitude, which denoted compulsory hard labour, was substituted by an Act of 1853.
19   Superintendent Registrar, Births, Deaths, Marriages, MWHB, Nenagh. Cause of death was 'old age and prostatic disease'.

Chapter 16
'To Remove the Mortal Remains'

In 1883, twenty-five years after the execution of the Cormacks, the County Gaol at Nenagh was reduced to the status of bridewell. Four years later the gaol was closed completely. All of the buildings, with the exception of two cell blocks, were acquired by the local community of the Sisters of Mercy for residential and school purposes.[1]

In a written account of the transfer of the gaol Mother Mary Catherine Cassidy revealed:

… from the time the possession of the gaol was obtained, numbers of men, from time to time asked permission to visit the Cormack grave. Many a fervent prayer was said there, and strong men were not ashamed to weep . . .[2]

However, no record of any commemoration ceremonies has surfaced – not even on the fiftieth anniversary of their execution, 11 May 1908.

Ireland had undergone major social, political and cultural changes during the last quarter of the nineteenth century. One notable change was the upsurge of the former peasant class to prominent positions in politics and local government under an advanced nationalist banner.

The United Irish League (UIL), the agrarian organisation founded in 1898 by William O'Brien and closely allied to the Irish Parliamentary Party under the leadership of John Redmond, MP, was a growing influence at the turn of the century. The passage of Wyndham's Land Act in 1903 paved the way for outright purchase by tenants of their holdings. Thereafter the UIL became very active in exploiting the terms of the Act, and in supporting tenants whose purchase negotiations with their landlords were not proceeding smoothly.

UIL branches were widespread in County Tipperary when, towards the end of 1908, disputes arose between the landlords and tenants of three large estates in the Thurles-Templemore area: those of Charles Neville Clarke, Graiguenoe, Holycross, Sir John Carden, Templemore, and Colonel Fitzgibbon Trant, JP, DL, Dovea House.[3]

Colonel Trant, who was a son of John Trant the employer of the murdered John Ellis, was foreman of the Tipperary (NR) grand jury in 1908. Trant's

Dovea House

tenants had withheld the rent in November of that year. In January 1909 they made him an offer to purchase for the equivalent of twenty years rent, and to pay the rent arrears less six shillings in the pound. He refused to sell on those terms. The report of this dispute in the *Nenagh News & Tipperary Vindicator*, included a short history of the Trant estate. It included references to the Ellis killing and the 'judicial murder on perjured evidence' of William and Daniel Cormack.[4]

Early in February 1909 a large demonstration was held in a field near the village of Loughmore. Its purpose was to enter a strong protest against Colonel Trant's refusal, and to 'enter into combination with tenants of Sir John Carden, Charles Clarke and all other landlords who refuse to sell'. Tension increased two weeks later when eight young men from Holycross district were arrested for 'riotous and disorderly conduct' in the vicinity of the Clarke estate.[5]

Attempts at a local boycott came to light when three members of Loughmore UIL were arrested in early March. They were taken to Templemore and charged with employing intimidatory tactics by ordering certain shopkeepers in Thurles not to supply goods to certain employees of Colonel Trant. Two of the defendants were sent for trial and one was discharged.[6]

The Trant dispute came to a head on 30 March 1909 when Colonel Trant sought ejectments against fourteen of his tenants at Thurles quarter sessions.[7] The judge said he had no hesitation in granting the decrees. However, both

Carden and Trant reached 'amicable arrangements' with their tenants in June.[8]

In the light of the foregoing, it is reasonable to conclude that the motivation behind the move in 1910 to have the remains of William and Daniel Cormack exhumed and publicly re-buried was partly humanitarian and partly political. While committed to a dignified public funeral, the organisers also intended it to be a display of nationalist strength centred on the United Irish League. Realisation of these ambitions was aided in no small way by the popular belief that the Cormacks had been hanged for a crime they did not commit. That the whole venture proceeded smoothly and with minimal conflict, was due largely to the skills of the two main players – John Walsh, auctioneer, Templemore, and James O'Brien, solicitor, Nenagh.

First Moves

From two files of correspondence relating to the re-burial, and from contemporary personal letters, it is possible to reconstruct the steps taken to secure the exhumation order and organise the funeral.[9]

Towards the end of March 1909 Sergeant Patrick Somers, of the Royal Irish Constabulary (RIC), stationed in Loughmore, sent the following report to his District Inspector, George L. Hildebrand, in Templemore. The report identifies the UIL as the prime instigators of the exhumation.

However, the fact that most of the cell blocks in the gaol were being demolished to make way for a new girls national school was probably the immediate cause of the initial impulse. The report by the local sergeant, quoted overleaf, confirms the concern of the Loughmore residents. They may have felt that the burial area was at risk from further development then or at a later date.

A meeting of this [Loughmore] branch of the United Irish League was held here yesterday morning. Rev Thomas Hackett, PP, presided and left before the meeting was over. The secretary, treasurer and two members of the committee were present. John Walsh and a man named Fitzgerald from Templemore were also present. The dispute between Colonel Trant, Dovea, was discussed. It was decided, I am informed, to have the remains of the two brothers Cormack, that were hanged in Nenagh years ago for the murder of Mr Ellis, agent to the present Col. Trant's father, removed from Nenagh.

All the branches in the district in Tipperary were to be written to with the purpose of raising funds for the purpose and with having different branch representatives and bands.

PS: I am informed that it is intended to remove the remains on 13th May next.
DI Hildebrand was amazed, and told Somers:

This is a very extraordinary intention. Are you quite sure your information is reliable? Is it the intention of the persons making the suggestion to carry it out in order to provoke hostility towards Col Trant? I am not sure if it will be possible for anybody to obtain permission.

Within a few days Sergeant Somers had the full story.

I beg to report that the remains of the Cormacks are to be taken here for burial. Every person in the sub-district has it that on May 11th [1909] next their remains will be taken to Loughmore. I am told that it was on the 11th May that they were executed at Nenagh ... It appears that a school is to be built on the place where they were buried and that is partly why they want to remove the remains. I do not see it is directly to invoke hostility towards Col. Trant that this is being done but if carried out it will bring him doubly before the public. I am also told that the bands are to practise the dead march in order to be able to play it at the funeral. I do not know if they will be allowed to remove the remains but as far as I can gather it is in contemplation. It is a long time yet and we will be able to ascertain further facts about this matter. I will keep in close touch with it.

A few days later again, 4 April 1909, Somers reported that 'as far as I can gather it is their intention to carry this out if they get permission to remove the remains'. Hildebrand now brought the County Inspector's (CI) office in Nenagh up to date – even though he considered it 'unnecessary to go to government in regard to a hypothetical matter only'. But he did stress that if the CI had any discretion in the matter, authority should be withheld until the dispute between Trant and his tenants was over. The County Inspector, John Matthew Galwey Foley, was confident 'that the authority to remove the remains will be asked but not given'.[10]

It was no 'hypothetical matter'. On 16 April 1909, John Walsh, auctioneer, Templemore, and chairman of that town's branch of the United Irish League, wrote to James O'Brien, solicitor, Nenagh:

The friends of the brothers Cormack ... are eager to gather their remains out of the graves in which they were placed by the Executioner. Will you please inform me must they get an order exhuming these corpses and from whom and what plan would you suggest for doing so?'

John Walsh, aged fifty-nine, conducted a widely-known auctioneering business which he had founded in 1883. Walsh had a high profile in

nationalist circles through his membership of the Irish Republican Brotherhood (IRB), and from the Land League agitation of the 1880s-90s during which he had been imprisoned as a 'suspect'. He was a member of Templemore Town Commissioners and its successor, the Urban District Council.

James O'Brien expressed his willingness to help immediately. At thirty years of age he was a generation younger than the auctioneer. He had a legal practice in Nenagh and had just been appointed Coroner for Tipperary North Riding.

Later that month Walsh forwarded to O'Brien the names of the next of kin on whose behalf the application to exhume was to be made – Thomas Cormack, Kilkillahara, and James Maher, Leugh, cousins of the Cormacks. Walsh stated that the parish priest of Loughmore, Very Rev. Canon Thomas Hackett, had given a special site for the graves, 'above which it is intended to raise a monument'. Walsh's letter concluded:

In the beginning at least it may be best not to give a political hue to the application to the Home Secretary – but after permission is granted we will have the biggest funeral procession that ever left Nenagh. I hope I am not predicting too soon . . .[12]

PERMISSION SOUGHT

In July 1909, too late for the anniversary originally targeted according to Sergeant Somers, James O'Brien applied to Chief Secretary Augustine Birrell, Dublin Castle, for an exhumation order. He also wrote to the Prisons Board. The letters created a stir and the Solicitor General's advice was sought. He decreed that the Lord Lieutenant could give no order to disinter a body but that he could 'direct that it be disinterred', adding:

The present case is, however, peculiar in its implication in being based on the grounds that the two men executed were innocent, a contention which of course government could not admit without proof. On the other hand the prison premises have been vested in the County Council since 1904 so that the application might be dealt with on ordinary grounds apart from the execution of the men. ...[13]

However, none of this useful information was conveyed to James O'Brien – only a brief note to the effect 'that the Chief Secretary has no authority to make any order in the matter'. The Lord Lieutenant, John Campbell, Earl of Aberdeen, replied likewise. Both were curt and to the point and offered no suggestion as to who had the authority.[14]

The Prisons Board reply of 20 August was more forthcoming:

... having regard to the fact that the entire Prison premises were handed over to the County Tipperary (N.R.) County Council in 1904, the Board do not appear to have any *locus standi* in the matter.[15]

Around this time too the RIC Inspector-General sent instructions to County Inspector, J. M. Galwey Foley, based in Nenagh, to report on any developments he had learned of the mooted exhumation and re-burial.[16]

In October 1909 James O'Brien made a formal application to the County Council, on behalf of the dead men's cousins, for permission to enter the former gaol grounds for the purpose of exhuming the remains. O'Brien, through John Walsh, had arranged that a resolution to that effect would be proposed by a member of the Council. The Council made the following Order.

That as far as the leave of this Council, as owners in fee of the Nenagh gaol burial ground, to comply with Mr O'Brien's request, is concerned, same is hereby granted unanimously with application to be made to the Trustees for the Sisters of Mercy who are lessees of said premises. [17]

In the course of the discussion at the meeting, a Council surveyor, Robert P. (Bertie) Gill, remarked that 'the nuns have kept the graves very nice and erected a nice cross over them' (opposite).

The *Nenagh News* of 20 November described it as '... an application that has no precedent in any county'.[18]

Most Rev. Michael Fogarty, Bishop of Killaloe, one of the Trustees for the Sisters of Mercy's property, was subsequently approached and gave the necessary consent for the grounds to be entered. The exhumation story also got mention in the *Irish Times*. [19]

In mid-November 1909 James O'Brien wrote to the Home Secretary in Whitehall, London, seeking permission to open the graves and 'take the remains for interment in the burial grounds'. The letter was sent back to Dublin to be dealt with. Accordingly, O'Brien was informed on 21 December that 'His Excellency is advised that he has no authority to give any permission in the matter, but His Excellency does not think it necessary he should interfere with the proposed action of the relatives'.[20]

In February 1910 O'Brien wrote at length to John Walsh to the effect that neither the Home Secretary nor Lord Lieutenant would be making any objections to the removal. It was O'Brien's own opinion, which he had confirmed by independent legal advice, that the authorities could make no objection 'even if they so desire', but he cautioned:

At the same time if it were to go to the ears of the Authorities that the exhumation of the remains was to be the occasion of anything like a political demonstration I will not answer for what action they may attempt to take ... It can be so couched as to fulfil your object without having on the face of it any political tinge and when you come to publish a Notice you ought to send a draft of it to me for approval, but at present do not publish anything ... I shall have to attend a meeting of the Urban District Council here tonight to get their formal consent to the exhumation as they are the Sanitary Authority of the District.[21]

That consent to exhume the remains was duly obtained from the UDC and in a letter written later that month O'Brien gave John Walsh the go-ahead to make the necessary funeral arrangements. Though O'Brien felt confident that the Council's ownership and the Sisters of Mercy occupation of the gaol premises were safeguards against any intervention by the authorities, at the same time he was against giving '... the Crown too much time to think over the matter', so he advised 'not to make the arrangements too much in advance'.[22]

However, unbeknownst to James O'Brien, the plans were known to the local police. This can be gleaned from Sergeant J. Donovan's report to

Members of the Organising Committee taken in front of the former gaol entrance in 1910. **Back** (l to r): John Walsh, District Surveyor, Thurles; Patrick Connolly, Baronstown; Patrick Barry, Kilnaseer; John Walsh, Hon. Secretary, Templemore; Con Moloney, Thurles; James Maher (Flood), Leugh, cousin of the Cormacks; Andy Callanan, Thurles; Thomas Cormack, Killahara, cousin. **Seated:** Patrick Egan, Killahara; James Russell, Ballyduag, Hon. Treasurer; Thomas Gleeson, Ballybristy; Ed Maher (Flood), Leugh, cousin; William Doyle, Coolegraine.

CI Foley on 12 February. '... that the 11th of May next, the anniversary of the executions has been fixed for the removal of the remains. ... It is probable that a <u>very large</u> number of persons will assemble on the occasion.'[23]

COMMITTEE FORMED

In early March 1910 a Committee, whose members were drawn from the parishes of Loughmore, Templemore and Thurles, was formally established. An appeal for subscriptions to fund the funeral and proposed memorial was prepared for circulation. It was published in local newspapers and 200 posters were printed.

The appeal was signed by Rev. Thomas Hackett, P.P., Loughmore, Chairman; James Russell, District Councillor, Ballyduag, Treasurer; John Walsh, Poor Law Guardian, Templemore, Hon. Secretary. It was stated that the funeral would coincide with 'the next anniversary of the executions', i.e. 11 May.[24]

James O'Brien continued to keep a watchful eye on the arrangements. He advised John Walsh to recommend to his Committee that the language in a draft circular sent for his approval should be toned down. The advice was taken and the idea of a circular dropped in favour of personal calls 'on League branches to solicit their aid and co-operation in the work'.

Committee activities and the appearance of posters inevitably confirmed what the local police already suspected – that this was going to be no ordinary funeral. Heffernan F. Consedine, the Deputy Inspector-General of the Constabulary, Dublin Castle, responded to the realisation that a public demonstration was contemplated by deciding that the County Inspector should see James O'Brien

and warn him on behalf of the relatives that no demonstration can be permitted and that an undertaking must be given that the exhumation and removal of the remains will be carried out as soon as convenient in as private a manner as possible and before the anniversary of the executions.[25]

Consedine had sent this decision to CI Foley with a note saying, 'you will I am sure discharge this duty tactfully and with discretion, but make the decision reached quite clear to the gentleman'.

The CI did as directed, was asked by O'Brien to put it in writing, which he did. The O'Brien response was then sent by Foley to Dublin. Consedine added this additional information before passing it up the line:

I am not aware and I cannot say whether anything came to light at any later stage to cast substantial doubt on the parties of that conviction but I do recall hearing as a boy that a popular belief existed that the two were innocent. Why I am sure I do not know but I have the idea that this rested largely on the allegation of the accused that the judge at the trial was very antagonistic to the extent even of being unfair. This is very likely a popular error. But the affair is now ancient history … There is little objection we can take to the removal to consecrated ground provided it be done in a private and dignified manner. [26]

O'BRIEN VERSUS DUBLIN CASTLE

James O'Brien's reply to CI Galwey Foley of 16 March 1910 was polite but firm.

Referring to your letter of 14th inst relative to the proposed exhumation … I shall be glad to know what the Government understands as a 'demonstration' and what number of persons will, in the opinion of the Government, be required to constitute a 'demonstration'.

It is generally conceded that there was a miscarriage of justice in the case of these unfortunate men and the greatest sympathy has always been felt at their unhappy fate. This being so there can be no question that a large body of the public will be anxious to show respect for their memory by attending the exhumation and funeral. And I shall be obliged if the Government will kindly state on what grounds it proposes to interfere with such an assemblage.

We have been accustomed in this county to the proclamation of public meetings, but this, I think, is the first occasion upon which any Government has attempted to interfere with the right of an individual to show respect for the dead.

There can be no justification for the proposed action of the Government except it anticipates a riot or disturbance, and I beg to the assure the Government it very much misjudges the character of the people of this county if it deems them capable of doing anything unseemly on so solemn an occasion. The intended proceedings on the 11th May will be in reality a funeral long deferred. And the reverence which Irishmen have always shown their dead is the best assurance the Government can have that nothing unseemly will take place.

As to the date of the exhumations: Surely the anniversary of the executions of the brothers McCormack is the most fitting day upon which to remove their mortal remains to consecrated ground; doing so will lend an added solemnity to the occasion, and I am amazed that the Government should, in the words of your letter, 'require an undertaking that the exhumation and removal of the remains will be carried out as soon as convenient in as private a manner as possible and before the anniversary of the executions'.

I can give no such undertaking, and I am at a loss to assign a reason for the attitude of the Government unless it be that finding it inadvisable or impossible to veto the exhumation it desires to heap contumely upon memories which very many still hold dear.

My clients resent the suggestion that they should act, as it were, by stealth. They have no reason to be ashamed of the project they have in hand; they will carry it out in a manner respectful to the deceased and creditable to themselves.

They will not molest any man or class, but they will insist on the undoubted right of themselves, their friends and sympathisers to assemble and pay the last honours to the dead. On that occasion nothing regrettable can occur except the Government intervenes to provoke it, and in such event the blame must rest not upon the people but upon the Government itself.[27]

Dublin Castle officials sought legal opinion, one of which stated. '... as I understand in law the disinterment of human remains is not in itself unlawful if it is done decently'. It concluded with the observation that as the executions took place over fifty years previously, and the judge was dead for thirty years, 'it would not be a matter for present politics. It is no doubt to be regretted that there is to be a demonstration but it is very difficult to say that it will constitute an unlawful assembly'.[28]

The Ears of Dublin Castle

Police awareness heightened as the date of the intended funeral drew near. This is well illustrated in a communication from acting County Inspector, Ivan Henry Price, Nenagh, to the Inspector-General of the Constabulary, Dublin Castle, on 14 April 1910.

I beg to report that the movement to hold a great public funeral accompanied by a great number of bands is growing in this county. The local press advocate all bands are practising the funeral march for the occasion. I have been quietly endeavouring to ascertain the size the demonstration is likely to attain ... I mentioned the matter to Mr Michael Gleeson, Crown Solr than whom no one has a better knowledge of the people of North Tipperary. He told me that he was sure the demonstration would be a large one and that it would be conducted in an orderly and solemn manner as a funeral. It now has no political significance and is not aimed at any one individual and cannot affect matters in this county. The only thing which would give it significance would be to suppress it.

I understand that Mr James O'Brien, solr, Nenagh, who obtained the permission to exhume the bodies, has stated that the only intention of the demonstrators is to hold a solemn funeral and that no disorder will ensue.

I cannot state definitely yet how many police will be necessary to prevent this demonstration. It would probably be 300 to 400 and great disturbance might ensue.

If I may venture to express a personal opinion I would say that the less notice is taken of this funeral procession by the police the better. Just as in the case of the Manchester Martyrs demonstrations which became insignificant and died out in most places.

The previous file on this subject ... was a confidential communication to Mr Galwey Foley CI. I mentioned this matter to him immediately before his proceeding on leave and told him my views. He concurred and said I should bring the matter again under the Inspector-General's notice when I had made due enquiry. I am enquiring from the other districts as to the extent to which the bands and people in their districts intend to take part in this demonstration. However, on receipt of attached report I thought it better to state my opinion fully when submitting it.

The report has an unsigned endorsement: '[to] CI Nenagh, Who are these men and of what crime were they accused? Were they executed? Who are promoting the movement?'[29]

PLANNING APACE

Meanwhile, reports were coming in to the District Inspector's offices from various police barracks around North Tipperary giving projections on the number of people and bands from their districts who planned to attend the funeral.

'... at least between two and three thousand people ... with all available horses and vehicles'. Fife and drum bands from Holycross, Clareen, Ballycahill, Moyne and Littleton' (Thurles report). The Templemore DI was flabbergasted. 'Do you mean that 2,000 or 3,000 people will attend from this district alone. Surely this is not so?' The reply brought no consolation, '... from the information received and which I believe to be reliable about the number stated, at least two thousand people will attend. This number will <u>not</u> go to Nenagh but will meet the remains in various places en route to Loughmore'.

Cloughjordan reported that 80 to 100 people planned to attend, but no band. Newport reported that there would be no 'regular contingent representing the district', but that a good many people would attend individually. Borrisokane had no arrangements to report but, like Newport, it was expected that '50-60 individuals' would attend. [30]

Details of the collections carried out to defray the funeral expenses were also transmitted to the Dublin RIC headquarters.

The sum of £8 10s was collected. Mike Blake, Moyneard, Joseph Morrissey, Moynetemple, Laurence Flynn, Moynetemple and Thomas Flynn of Moyneard, all prominent members of the UIL, collected.

It was agreed to by the parties concerned to deduct £1 from this amount to defray the expense of Moyne fife and drum band going to Loughmore on the 11th May.

The people generally paid little attention to this collection and a great number gave no subscription. [Moyne]

I beg to report ... that a meeting was held here on the 14th inst. for the purpose of collecting funds for the above and to have the 11th May a general holiday in order that the townspeople might attend. The meeting was got up by the members of the Town Tenants League and included members of the Sinn Féin committee. The sum of 14*s* was collected but on the whole the people of the town are rather lukewarm about the matter and up to the present nothing definite has been arranged.

This also applies to Clonakenny where no arrangement has been made either to send a band or to attend in full numbers, but if the people get an invitation they will probably go with the band. [Roscrea]

I beg to report that a <u>collection was held</u> ... on 10th inst. near the Cathedral gates.

Posters were exhibited in almost all the shops windows in the town and also in conspicuous places in the town and vicinity announcing that a collection would be made and requesting the people to subscribe liberally.

A sum of £41 was subscribed by those who attended Divine Service on the date mentioned. The collectors were John Walsh, Assistant Co. Surveyor; D. H. Ryan, draper; James Maher, publican; Denis McCarthy, draper; Denis O'Keeffe, draper; Patrick Finn, publican; Patrick Darmody, Secretary UIL; John Ryan, publican; William Dwyer, cattle dealer, all of Thurles.[31]

Included with the above Thurles report was a poster with all the funeral arrangements. This shows organisational ability and attention to detail by the Committee, and a simple but effective way of communication. Three of the points were:

Bands attending are to play no tunes except one of the Dead Marches during the sad procession.

Each band who joins in the funeral procession is to take up at least 50 yards behind the preceding band.

Mourning emblems. It is hoped that all participating in this funeral will wear as a mourning badge as far as possible a piece of crape on the left arm tied with a small piece of green ribbon.

Meanwhile Deputy C.I. Price, Nenagh, compiled an answer to the question, 'who are these men ...', albeit mistakenly adding the prefix 'Mc' to the victims' surname and substituting the name 'William' for Ellis's first name John.

I beg to state that the brothers McCormack were two small farmers living on the Trant estate in the district of Templemore. They were tried at Nenagh Spring assizes 1858 before the late Judge Keogh. They were charged with the murder of William (sic) Ellis, a steward at the time in the Trant estate. The murder took place between Templemore and Dovea. Mr Ellis's driver was a party to the murder but his evidence was accepted as an informer. The murder was treated as agrarian. The

Cormacks were convicted and were hanged outside Nenagh gaol on 11th May 1858.

After the conviction a man named Gleeson, who also resided in or near the Trant estate, gave himself up to the Resident Magistrate in the district and stated that he, Gleeson, committed the murder. However, after investigation Gleeson was discharged and sentence on the McCormacks was carried out.

It is stated that Gleeson on his death bed in America adhered to his former confession and admitted that he alone committed the murder and that the McCormacks were innocent.

It is stated that Ellis had amoral relations with the McCormacks' sister and that was one reason why the McCormacks were suspected. On the other hand it is stated that Gleeson wanted to marry the McCormacks' sister and that he, Gleeson, therefore planned to murder Ellis.

It is intended to carry the remains of the McCormacks to Loughmore churchyard, Templemore district. Ellis was buried at Killahara, two and a half miles from Loughmore.

John Walsh, IRB suspect in Templemore, has taken a principal part in connection with the removal of the remains but Mr James O'Brien, Solr, Nenagh, Treasurer of the UILeague is the most active in the matter now which has been taken up generally now by even moderate men. When the move was first started about a year ago the trouble in the Trant estate was acute. This has however all settled down now. ...

The letter is annotated by Deputy Inspector-General Consedine:

The Inspector-General has already expressed an opinion on this matter to which he adheres and to which he has nothing to add. The relatives of these unfortunate McCormacks do not seem to be central in this affair, it is engineered by others partly, no doubt, through political and misapplied patriotic views and partly to bring themselves into prominence. We now learn (for the first time, I think), that Mr O'Brien, solicitor, who has been in communication with the Government, is the treasurer of the local branch of the UIL. The fact suggests an inference. [32]

It was now into the fourth week of April and so far James O'Brien had received no official confirmation that the funeral-cum-demonstration would be allowed to proceed unmolested by the police. 27 April brought a carefully worded letter on behalf of His Excellency, Lord Aberdeen, referring to O'Brien's reply to CI Foley and intimating:

While it is not possible for His Excellency to enter into discussion on the matter referred to therein I am to point out that the selection of the anniversary of the executions ... as the date of making the proposed removal ... and the holding of any demonstration in connection therewith, would be wholly at variance with His Excellency's interpretation of your letter of 23rd November 1909. [33]

James O'Brien had read between the lines. He knew that he had the authorities backtracking and he pressed home his advantage.

My clients did not select the anniversary of the execution of the McCormacks as the date for exhuming the remains with any sinister intention, nor can they even now understand what valid objection there is to the proposed exhumation on the 11th prox. My letter of the 23rd November last to the Home Secretary made no reference to the proposed date of exhumation, and I therefore must confess myself unable to understand how the Lord Lieutenant could interpret this letter as an undertaking that the remains would not be exhumed on that particular date.

With reference to 'demonstration' of which you make mention in your letter, this term has been applied by the Authorities to the proposed funeral but my clients altogether repudiate the suggestion that the exhumation and funeral will be made an occasion for anything in the nature of a 'demonstration'.

It is proposed to exhume the remains on the 10th prox and to deposit them overnight in the Catholic church here, to have High Mass celebrated on the following morning, and immediately after High Mass to have the remains conveyed to Loughmore churchyard. Unquestionably a large number of people will attend the ceremony at the church and the funeral for the purpose of showing their respect to the memory of the McCormacks, but His Excellency may rest assured that the occasion will be far too solemn in the minds of all concerned to permit the occurrence of anything which could offend the susceptibility of any person. The suggestion that anything of the nature indicated by your letter would occur is positively shocking to the feelings of those whom I represent, and unless the authorities, by unwise and uncalled for intervention, ferment a disturbance everything will be carried out in a manner of credit to those attending the funeral.

While it is right that I extend to your letter of the 26th inst. the courtesy of a reply I feel bound to direct your attention to the fact that in your letter of 21 December 1909 you stated, 'I am directed by the Lord Lieutenant to inform you that His Excellency is advised that he has no authority to give any permission in the matter'. This being so I desire most respectfully to say that if His Excellency had no authority to give permission to exhume it does not seem clear what authority he has to interfere with the arrangements connected with the exhumation. But, apart altogether from this, I, as already mentioned, can assure His Excellency that there will be no necessity whatever for his intervention. [34]

However, James O'Brien was not to know that the Lord Lieutenant's letter had been drafted by the Attorney-General, Redmond Barry, as a 'face saving' measure, since the A-G's opinion was that 'no objection to it ought to be pressed to the extent of taking any forcible action on the occasion'.

The A-G's legal opinion focused on two important facts. Firstly, that the authorities had not been fully apprised of the extent of the funeral by James

O'Brien and, secondly, that O'Brien might have interpreted the terms laid down by the authorities, as conveyed to him by CI Foley, to mean that force might be used if the terms of this letter were not met. The LL's letter took care of the first point, and an instruction of 6 May from the Inspector-General of Constabulary to Deputy CI Price, Nenagh, took care of the second one.

There would be no interference with the 'demonstration' if it takes place. The less notice the police take of the affair the better. No display of force. No police presence other than such as would be detailed for order duty on the occasion of the assemblage of a considerable number of people for an ordinary, peaceful purpose, presumably the local [police] force will be ample.[35]

NOTES

1   Nancy Murphy, *Walkabout Nenagh* (Nenagh 1994), p. 6. The Sisters moved their national school to the gaol buildings in 1887 and their convent to its Governor's House in 1888. Five of the gaol cell blocks and the women's prison were knocked to make way for a new school (1911) and a new convent (1913).

2   Mother Mary Catherine Cassidy (1833-1929), 'The Story of Nenagh Convent' in *Molua* 1953, p. 18.

3   *Nenagh News & Tipperary Vindictor* (hereafter *NN & TV*) 7 Nov 1908, 2 Jan 1909. Col. Fitzgibbon Trant was High Sheriff of Co. Tipperary in 1889. He died in 1912 aged 63 years and is buried beside his father John in the graveyard adjoining Killahara church in Dovea village. His son, Laurence Dominick Trant, sold Dovea House and adjoining estate in 1945 for £2,000 to the local co-operative. A few years later it was taken over by the South Eastern Cattle Breeding Society and as such continues. The Society published, in co-operation with Laurence's son Ion F., a memoir entitled *Just Across the Water* (Dovea 1996). Ion F. lived in Dovea House as a child and young adult and died in 1996.

4   *NN & TV*, 2 Jan 1909. It transpired at a later court hearing that Trant considered the offer 'as too ridiculous to consider'. He claimed in court that his offer of twenty-one and a half years' rent as the purchase price was not given consideration by the tenants.

5   *NN & TV*, 6 & 27 Feb 1909.

6   *NN & TV*, 6 Mar 1909. The men were Thomas Gleeson and Patrick Maher, Ballybreeda, Patrick Cormack, Tinvoher. Gleeson's and Maher's trial was postponed at the 1909 summer assizes because a witness was sick. Both were given continued bail.

7   *NN & TV*, 3 Apr 1909; *NG*, 3 April 1909.

8   *NN & TV*, 12 Jun, 17 Jul 1909. In the report of the settlement of the Carden and Trant disputes with tenants, details of the Carden settlement are given but not those for Trant.

9   NA, CSORP 1920/8218; Cormack file donated to Tipperary County Library by James O'Brien & Co., Solicitors, Nenagh; letters and other documents in the

possession of John Walsh's family, Templemore.

10 NA, CSORP 1920/8218. An official annotated Sergt Somers's first report, 'very far fetched', when it was eventually passed on to Dublin Castle.

11 Cormack file, Co Library, Thurles, John Walsh to James O'Brien, 16 Apr 1909.

12 ditto, Walsh to O'Brien, 27 Apr 1909.

13 O'Brien to Chief Sec. 10 Jul 1909; NA, CSORP 1920/8218, No. 1451.

14 NA, CSORP 1920/8218, No. 14728 – Chief Sec. & Lord Lieut to O'Brien, 11 Aug & 19 Aug 1909.

15 J. White, Prisons Board, to O'Brien, 20 Aug 1909.

16 NA, CSORP 1920/8218, No. 16101.

17 *NN & TV,* 20 Nov 1909.

18 *NN & TV,* 20 Nov 1909.

19 Cormack file, Co Library, Thurles, Dr Fogarty to O'Brien, 18 Nov 1909; *Irish Times*, 22 Nov 1909.

20 NA, CSORP 1920/8218, No. 2555,

21 O'Brien to Walsh, Feb 1910.

22 O'Brien to Walsh, 18 Feb 1910.

23 NA, CSORP 1920/8218, No. 2631.

24 Copy of appeal and poster in Cormack file, County Library, Thurles.

25 NA, CSORP 1920/8218, No. 2631.

26 ditto, No 4887.

27 NA, CSORP 1920/8218.

28 ditto, No.4887.

29 ditto, No. 54282.

30 ditto, Crime Special, No. 7557.

31 ditto, Crime Special, No. 7557. A poster was included with the report from Thurles.

32 ditto, No. 6950.

33 ditto, No. 4887.

34 ditto, No. 7615.

35 ditto, No. 8391.

Chapter 17
'A Funeral Long Deferred'

Meanwhile, the funeral organising committee had been drawing up route details and engaging bands to participate in the long journey from Nenagh to Loughmore. John Walsh had problems a-plenty, one of which he fielded to James O'Brien for adjudication. Some of the Committee had suggested that the funeral should go past the Cormacks' old home, but this meant going past the Trant estate also. It was not adverted to that it would mean passing by John Ellis's burial place too. Others were for avoiding that route. O'Brien favoured avoidance and this was agreed to.[1]

By the first week of May all arrangements were complete. John Dillon, MP, whose name was synonymous with successive land reform campaigns since the foundation of the Land League in 1879, had intimated to John Walsh that he would travel to Thurles by train on the 11th and go by car to Loughmore for the interment, after which he would address the crowd outside the church gates.[2]

On the evening of Monday 9 May 1910, members of the funeral organising committee, the Cormacks' cousins James Maher, Leugh, and Thomas Cormack, Killahara, clergy from Loughmore and Nenagh districts, members of the press and onlookers, all assembled in the grounds of the Convent of Mercy.

Among the onlookers were people who had witnessed the executions. One man present, named Matt McGrath, Shallee, Nenagh, in gaol in 1858, was said to have assisted in the removal of the bodies from the scaffold and at their burial afterwards.[3] The *Nenagh News* reported:

The remains were intact and all the teeth perfectly sound in the skull. The bones were in a perfect state of preservation and on the feet of William's skeleton were the nailed shoes worn at the time of execution. There was no trace of Daniel's shoes...

The report added that a local man [unnamed] in Nenagh had always claimed to be in possession of them.[4]

The remains were placed in two oak coffins and carried out through the entrance arch, above which the scaffold had been sited, and across the road to St Mary's of the Rosary, the town's R.C. church.

(above) **The Opening of the Grave**.

(l to r): Pat Egan, Killahara; Tom Gleeson, Ballybristy; James Maher (Flood), cousin of the Cormacks; Phil Gleeson, Ballybristy; Ed Maher (Flood), cousin; James Russell, Ballyduag; John Walsh, Surveyor, Thurles; Andrew Callanan, Leugh; John Walsh, Drom, clerk of works on the girls school then under construction in the gaol grounds; —; Thomas Cormack, Killahara, cousin; Paddy (Sonny) and Willie Hackett, Nenagh. The latter two had come seeking a priest for a christening.

The girls who figure in both pictures are probably pupils of the national school then located in the former gaol buildings.

(left) Daniel Cormack's remains being carried out through the former gaol entrance and below the glazed doors through which he came on to the scaffold.

Boys from Nenagh CBS escort one of the coffins to St Mary's of the Rosary church door. The bearers include Committee members. The ladies have not been identified but are probably wives and sisters of the Committee.

On Wednesday 11 May the day-long proceedings began with Requiem Mass at 11 o'clock, attended by clergy from Nenagh and surrounding parishes and from Loughmore. Then the two hearses, each drawn by two black-clad horses with white head plumes, set out on the 22-mile journey.

All Nenagh's shops were shuttered and thousands of people lined the streets. Walking ahead of the hearses were the CBS boys and members of Nenagh Urban District Council. Behind the hearses came members of the United Irish League, other public bodies, Nenagh Brass Band with craped instruments and muffled drums; Templemore Brass Band; the general public, outside cars, carriages, traps, carts and horsemen, interspersed with brass and reed and fife and drum bands playing funeral marches. The photograph opposite shows the funeral in Castle (now Pearse) St.

Deputy County Inspector Price was able to send a report to Dublin that the funeral took one hour to pass the RIC barracks, that it left Nenagh at 1 o'clock and that all was 'most orderly'. Templemore DI's report was in a similar tone – 10,000 persons assembled in the town, all quiet and orderly, a few cases of drunkenness but no 'breach of the peace'.[5]

147

(below): One of the hearses passing through the enormous crowd gathered in Borrisoleigh's main street. The assorted vehicles, with drivers and passengers, joined the funeral procession for the drive to Loughmore, some eight miles distant.

The *Nenagh News* estimated that 10,000 persons marched in the funeral procession and that 20 bands participated, and that participants, including onlookers, reached an estimated 50,000. Extra crowds joined in or viewed the cortege at cross-roads and premier vantage points on the route. Thousands lined the streets of Borrisoleigh and banners were displayed on most of the shops. Photographs of the funeral were taken at various points, to be later sold as postcards.

In Templemore the funeral was led through the town by an estimated 300 cyclists walking in formation alongside their machines.

The event was a funeral, displaying the inherent neighbourliness in sympathy with the victims of a tragedy. It was also the political demonstration forecast by John Walsh and feared by the authorities. The participants were the sons and grandsons of the downtrodden of 1858, now on a rising tide thanks to three decades of land reform. This was as recent as the fruits of significant acts of parliament of 1903 and 1909 with their emphasis on enabling the purchase of their holdings by the tenant farmers. One of their leaders in the agitation of those decade was to be the post-funeral speaker, John Dillon, MP for Mayo and formerly for Tipperary.

The cortege went past the railway station to approach Loughmore via the townland of Cloone and Penane Cross – coincidentally, the same route John Ellis had taken on that fateful night in 1857.

In Loughmore the coffins were shouldered into the church. Following prayers, a sermon was preached by Fr Hackett, PP, the chairman of the organising committee. His sermon was carried in full by the local newspapers. He chose his words and allusions carefully so as not to be seen as condoning the murder, while at the same time interpreting a probable rationale for it. He put on record the local tradition as regards who the real murderer was. He said that the murderer had been 'under notice by Ellis to quit his holding'. However, Fr Hackett did not identify him by name.

The innocence of the Cormacks of the murder of Mr Ellis is certain from the testimony of the man who perpetrated the deed. He frequently during his life admitted the crime, and always exonerated the brothers from participation, direct or indirect, in its commission. And there is, moreover, independent and conclusive evidence that he was the assassin. He had the 'agrarian' motive for the murder. ... And he had the moral motive for the murder. That motive for him was the determining one. It is certain that Ellis was immoral. And the man who had murdered him believed he [Ellis] had made adulterous advances towards his sister, the wife of a person connected with the estate of which Ellis was the factor.[6]

John Dillon, MP, was the only other speaker. Careful to keep the funeral

Loughmore church grounds on the day of the funeral.

non-political, he was confined to addressing the crowd after the religious ceremonies were completed and *outside* the church gate. The content of his speech can be viewed in the light of these qualities identified by his biographer: ' a hatred of servility, whether towards Church or State; an almost instinctive understanding of the needs and desires of Irishmen in general and of Irish countrymen in particular; an extraordinary flair for political calculation and analysis.'[7]

Some of his rhetoric was probably 'political calculation' directed at the hearts and votes of an audience. The background was the arrival of a new government that January with a knife-edged majority and the Irish Party holding a balance of power while focused on Home Rule for Ireland; a strong possibility of another election later that year; the loss of a couple of the Party's MPs to a new party called Sinn Féin.[8]

I say it is fitting that now, after the expiry of these fifty-two years, on the anniversary of that dreadful legal crime, that the bones of these men should be brought to rest with their people and their fathers. And it is fitting that it should be done at a time when the hateful and the accursed system which was guilty of their murder and the murder of hundreds of our people is tottering to its final fall (applause). ...

I say and maintain that all the crime of Ireland, with very few exceptions, is the result, and the direct result – and I might almost say the inevitable result – of the persecution and the extermination of this system ... we look forward to a brighter future, when it will not be in the power of any man like Ellis to throw down the roof-trees as he did (applause). They thought to exterminate the people of Tipperary; they tried to exterminate the people of Tipperary and of Ireland; to exterminate the old race from the soil of Ireland. ...

The O'Donoghue, who was then member for this county, called attention to the matter in the House of Commons, but the government refused to produce young Burke's evidence, and they, of course, spirited him away out of the country. ...

Tipperary today has acquitted them of every stain upon their memory, and instead of being ashamed of the Cormack Brothers, Tipperary is proud of them (great cheering).[9]

The funeral organisers had taken a decision to make a unique break with tradition as regards the actual burial. The two coffins were not put in graves in the normal way, but were placed in a vault below ground level. The coffins were left free-standing and open to view – as they still are today.

Local subscriptions towards the cost of the funeral and memorial were supplemented by remittances from emigrants in Australia, Canada and the United States. Many were sent to the *Nenagh News* or *Tipperary Star* with sympathetic letters. The extensive coverage given by both papers to the funeral had included summarised accounts of the trial and execution.[10] The *Cork Examiner* carried a special photographic supplement.[11]

The account of the funeral expenses presented to John Walsh, Hon. Secretary of the organising committee, by Edward Mullaly, Templemore, shows the cost to have been £67 8*s*. 3*d*., the equivalent of an approximate £4,500 in late 1997 money values, summarised as follows:

the supply of 2 massive oak coffins, lined and mounted with solid brass mounting, including breast plates engraved . . . 2 hearses with 4 horses and heavily draped, 3 carriages with horses draped . . . overnight lodgings and payment for the drivers, dinner for guests and Committee.[12]

James O'Brien gave his protracted legal service free of charge. The legal practice he founded has its offices at his one-time residence, 30 Castle/Pearse Street, Nenagh, still under his name and six doors from its 1910 address. He died in 1963 at the age of 83 years. He had served as State solicitor for North Tipperary for some decades. He was one of the five men who purchased the *Nenagh Guardian* newspaper in 1916 and changed its policy to an avowedly nationalist one.

John Walsh died in 1929, aged 78 years. His name also continues on the auctioneering business in Templemore, later conducted by his son Paul and now by his grandson, John G. Walsh

Within a few years the Cormack vault was enhanced by the addition of an overground decorative surround, and steps down to an entrance chamber in which were erected two marble wall tablets, the work of John Bracken & Son, Templemore. One recorded the funeral ceremony. Its Latin inscription is taken from Ecclesiasticus, 44:14. The second one records the circumstances of their trial and execution. Its Latin inscription is taken from Wisdom, 3: 2,3. There are two misprints in the lettering: *corum* should read *eorum*; *insipientum* should read *insipientium*.

IN COMMEMORATION OF THE REMOVAL
OF THE REMAINS OF THE
CORMACK BROTHERS FROM THE JAILYARD
AT NENAGH TO THIS MAUSOLEUM ON MAY 11TH 1910
IN THE MORNING A SOLEMN REQUIEM OFFICE
AND HIGH MASS WERE CELEBRATED IN THE
PARISH CHURCH, NENAGH, CANON MCMAHON
PRESIDING, AND AN IMMENSE NUMBER OF
KILLALOE PRIESTS BEING IN THE CHOIR,
THE FUNERAL CORTEGE, WHICH CONTAINED
MR JOHN DILLON, M.P.; MR J. HACKETT, M.P.;
AND MANY OTHERS OF HIGH NAME AND
INSPIRING EXAMPLE, WAS BY MAGNITUDE,
REPRESENTATIVENESS AND OBSERVANCE
    UNPRECEDENTED IN IRELAND.
AT LOUGHMORE, THE PASTOR PREACHED
A FUNERAL ORATION AND ASSISTED BY
    PRIESTS FROM IRELAND, ENGLAND,
AMERICA AND AUSTRALIA, OFFICIATED AT
THE PLACING OF THE REMAINS HERE TO
REST IN PEACE AND HONOUR UNTIL
THE DAY OF THEIR VINDICATION BY
JESUS CHRIST BEFORE THE WHOLE
HUMAN RACE IN THE
VALLEY OF JOSOPHAT.

"CORPORA SANCTORUM IN PACE
SEPULTA SUNT: ET VIVENT NOMINA
CORUM IN AETERNAM. R.I.P.

John Bracken & Son

This Latin inscription translates as:
THE BODIES OF THE HOLY ONES ARE BURIED IN PEACE,
    AND THEIR NAMES SHALL LIVE FOR ETERNITY. REST IN PEACE

BY THE IRISH RACE IN MEMORY OF THE BROTHERS
DANIEL AND WILLIAM CORMACK,
WHO FOR THE MURDER OF A LAND AGENT NAMED
ELLIS, WERE HANGED AT NENAGH,
AFTER SOLEMN PROTESTATION BY EACH ON THE
SCAFFOLD OF ABSOLUTE AND ENTIRE INNOCENT
OF THAT CRIME, THE 11TH DAY OF MAY 1858. THE
TRAGEDY OF THE BROTHERS OCCURRED
THROUGH FALSE TESTIMONY PROCURED BY
GOLD AND TERROR; THE ACTION, IN THEIR
TRIAL, OF JUDGE KEOGH – A MAN, WHO
CONSIDERED PERSONALLY, POLITICALLY,
RELIGIOUSLY AND OFFICIALLY, WAS ONE OF
THE MONSTERS OF MANKIND; AND THE
VERDICT OF A PREJUDICED, PARTISAN,
PACKED PERJURED JURY. CLEAR PROOF
OF THE INNOCENCE OF THE BROTHERS
AFFORDED BY ARCHBISHOP LEAHY
TO THE VICEROY OF THE DAY, BUT HE,
NEVERTHELESS, GRATIFIED THE APPETITE
OF A BIGOTED, EXTERMINATING AND
ASCENDANCY CASTE, BY A JUDICIAL
MURDER OF THE KIND WHICH LIVES
BITTERLY AND PERPETUALLY IN A
NATION'S REMEMBRANCE

"VISI SUNT OCULIS INSIPIENTUM
MÓRI: ILLI; AUTEM SUNT IN PACE.

R.I.P.

John Bracken & Son
Templemore

THEY DID SEEM IN THE EYES OF THE UNWISE TO DIE
BUT THEY ARE IN PEACE
REST IN PEACE

In 1949 a committee, comprised mainly of sons and relatives of the 1910 one, undertook to raise funds for necessary conservation work and repairs. These included some changes to the overground surround and varnishing of the coffins.[13] Just as the graves had attracted sympathisers to the old gaol grounds in Nenagh so does their resting place in Loughmore, now cared for by the parish.

A VOICE FROM THE GRAVE

The administration of the day, or indeed later administrations, never declared that the Cormacks had been wrongfully convicted.

However, newspaper reports of the re-burial brought to light a hitherto unrecounted story endorsing the Cormacks' own claim of innocence and was the nearest thing to the much-reviled Judge Keogh speaking from the grave.

The *Nenagh News* of May 1910 carried a letter from Canon John McMahon, P.P., Nenagh, to the effect that he had received a letter from a priest friend in Kerry recounting an incident which had occurred in Tralee thirty-four years previously, 1876. It concerned the trial of a Merchant Navy Captain charged with the murder of an apprentice seaman.

The evidence was strong against the prisoner, wrote the Kerry priest, and everyone saw from the first sentence of Judge Keogh's charge that he was satisfied that the prisoner was guilty of murder ... To the last sentence of his charge he charged for murder, when suddenly, to the amazement of all he said 'Gentlemen of the jury, after all, perhaps a verdict of manslaughter would meet the requirements of the case'.

The priest, apparently mystified by this change of mind, mentioned it to a legal acquaintance, Sir John Neligan, who had been present at the trial. The answer he got was:

... In a conversation I had with him [Judge Keogh] last night ... I referred to it. 'It is as you say', said the Judge, 'I became suddenly frightened at the last moment. I hanged two Tipperary men who were innocent. They have been haunting me ever since and at the end of my charge they came up before me. What could I do?'[14]

NOTES

1   Walsh to O'Brien 26 & 29 Apr 1910.
2   John Dillon to John Walsh, 8 May 1910.
3   *NN & TV,* 14 May 1910.
4   ditto.
5   NA, CSORP 1920/8218, No. 16101/31001.
6   *Tipperary Star,* 21 May 1910.
7   F. S. L. Lyons, *John Dillon* (London 1968), p. 482.
8   Michael Bentley, *Politics Without Democracy* (London 1984), pp. 354-6; Lyons
    cited above, p. 299.
9   *Nenagh News,* 14 May 1910.
10 *NN &TV, TS,* 14 May & 8 October 1910 – $105 was sent from Chicago.
11 The photographs were taken by Lewy Gleeson, solicitor, 20 Summerhill, Nenagh.
12 Original in John Walsh papers.
13 Copy of original specification presented to author by the late Paul Walsh,
    Templemore, son of John Walsh.
14 *NN &TV,* 28 May 1910.

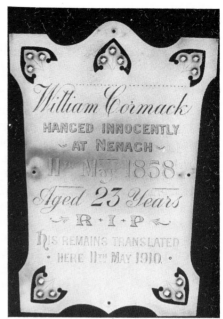

(below): The two coffins in the vault.

(above): The brass plaques on the coffins. The 1910 Funeral Committee who had them inscribed seems to have had the same difficulty as obtains in 1997 in establishing the brothers' exact ages.

Chapter 18
Conclusion?

The chances of a Parliamentary Inquiry being conceded in 1858 were slim. The fate of victims who were 'only two Tipperary peasants', in the emotive phrase of the Irish MP (p. 105), was of lesser consequence than the sympathy, proper in itself, for the initial victim, Ellis. The murder was yet another instance of an attack on landed property and its dominant interests. And it had occurred in 'Turbulent Tipperary'. The family of Prime Minister Edward Stanley, Earl of Derby, had almost 7,000 acres there and in adjoining Co. Limerick. Their agent had been threatened in 1842 with the fate of a landlord murdered a month previously.[1] Potential evictions from the lands were looming as a topic of publicity in the late 1850s.[2] The grant of an inquiry would have opened up what another administration in more recent times termed 'an appalling vista'– of a possible miscarriage of justice engineered by the very system on which justice for all classes depended.

It seems appropriate for an historical enquiry, fourteen decades on, to focus on the questions which might have been addressed if allowed by a more open regime in the 1850s or 1860s. The evidence that exists is referenced below to the page numbers in the text, for example: (105)

The aspects of the case to be questioned seem to fall as follows: • whether the members of the grand jury were right to send the Cormacks for trial; • the conduct of the investigation as revealed in the trials; • the conduct of the trials by prosecution, defence and presiding judge; • the quality of the evidence and consequently whether the second trial jury was justified in their verdict; • whether there were grounds for appeal, for a case stated by the judge for judgement by the superior court, and ultimately for mercy by the Lord Lieutenant.
• Finally, and leaving the law aside, has the widespread belief in the Cormacks' innocence been justified or might they have been guilty after all?

Was the Grand Jury Guilty

of sending forward a bill of indictment which they should have rejected, arising from any 'long-cherished prejudices' (108)? The answer must be: 'Not guilty'. They had before them the sworn evidence of an accomplice (49-51) and its corroboration as to identification of the accused by the murdered man's driver (52). In adverting to these they had been properly instructed by Judge Keogh (37). It was not their function to raise a question in law as to Burke's acceptability as corroborator nor to cross-check the evidence in detail which would have been in effect engaging in a paper trial.

158

of 'rather a desire to punish someone than a determination to discriminate carefully between the innocent and the guilty' (103)? Firstly, one has to say that the RMs, Jones and Goold, fairly enough focused initially on the potential 'private revenge' motive (14); Ellis's reputation, as outlined by Samuel Cooke (29), justifies this. His alleged involvement with Catherine Cormack, whether slanderous gossip or genuine knowledge, put the Cormacks among possible suspects. However, other local knowledge as regards land trouble, evidenced by Cooke (26) and by landlord Trant (48, 60), would surely have warranted other suspects being detained for examination. In that regard, defence counsel Rolleston's vehement questions on the possibilities of land trouble being the motive (63) appear justified. Does one then conclude that the RMs were too limited in their enquiries and therefore negligent? The defence counsel's assertion that Mr Jones seemed to forget his basic duty 'to ascertain the truth' (121) is pertinent. RM Goold must share in that assessment.

Jones was emphatic in the Anne Brophy false imprisonment case that she had not denied knowing the alleged third person in the gossipy yard (118) and thence that she was withholding evidence and justified his several renewals of detention. But Rolleston's charge that he was overstretching the law is valid.

The threat alleged by that dubious witness Burke – that Jones told him, 'You may stop in gaol till you rot' (53) – is serious. In the Anne Brophy case, of course, Jones denied saying so and amplified this by telling of a previous denial to the clerk Carmichael during the trial. But it was at least casual, if he did deny it to Carmichael, that he did not ensure that the prosecuting counsel were made aware of it by the clerk.

Which brings one to Attorney-General Whiteside. If Carmichael was grossly negligent and did not pass on the reply, Whiteside and his team should have followed up their query with Jones himself. If Carmichael did pass on Jones's denial, the prosecution now had grounds for suspecting that Burke had perjured himself in front of their eyes. Should they have informed the judge, cross-examined Jones privately, or go so far as to immediately withdraw the case on the grounds that a key witness was a liar?

The possibility dawns that Whiteside was here guilty of professional misconduct. One adverts to Chief Baron Pigot's reminiscence, during the Anne Brophy case, of his own honourable role on the part of the Crown in a trial (123). Perhaps Pigot, 'a most scrupulous and conscientious judge'[3], was being more pointed than merely anecdotal.

Otherwise, Whiteside's apologia for making a tough case during the trial is conventional and acceptable (84). However, his introduction without notice to the defence of the evidence of the gaoler-eavesdropper Sadleir (54, 62) fully earned Rolleston's trenchant denunciations (65). He misled parliament later (102-6) by withholding the fact that the escorting policemen verified car-driver Gleeson's account of the Burke 'confession'.

The Evidence

One dismisses all the evidence as regards the punchings as inconclusive (48, 51, 61 & 64). The lodger Callaghan's evidence on comings and goings in the house (54, 61-2) was flatly contradicted by his own wife and by Catherine Cormack (53, 62), even if theirs was negative evidence. It was well covered by Rolleston's closing speech (64), pointing out in effect that the occupants would have heard three openings and closings of the door if Spillane's evidence were correct. Rolleston might have added, and perhaps did but was unreported, that Spillane's departure within minutes of Callaghan's retiring to his own room could have accounted for the one opening and closing of the door, and that if the prosecution was correct there would have been yet another within the hour due to the return of the brothers from their alleged deed.

The sorry figure which Sadleir cut in the Anne Brophy case (121-2) gives only hindsight vis-a-vis the Cormacks' trials. His evidence at those trials appears to have been discounted by Keogh in his summing up (68).

Spillane and Burke

That the prosecution brought forward an unstable, hysterical youth in Spillane is extraordinary. Even allowing for the pressure he was under during incisive cross-examination there were notable self-contradictions: prepared to fire the shot if asked – might go again – not prepared to commit a murder himself (51, 60); Ellis beating him but not having a dispute (50); the love of justice as against saving his own neck (51).

Burke's whole role in the affair is fairly summarised by Rolleston (62-3) and in the Leahy petition (80-1) as well as in the Cormacks' petition (79). Even a 'soft youth' (46) could hardly be excused for his fore-knowledge, if his evidence in that respect were true, and failure both to alert Ellis and to seek his protection. The basic point is well made that his sworn evidence at the inquest (16) and his sworn evidence at the trials (52-4, 60-1) are incompatible. As to why he was not put on trial for aiding and abetting a murder, 'a principal in the second degree': the appalling conclusion can only be that he was needed by the prosecution to corroborate Spillane, though in essence an accomplice and thereby bereft of corroborating value. Burke's bizarre week of conversations with his driver and escort en route from Nenagh to Roscrea and his total denial of them under examination by Deputy-Inspector Brownrigg (93-8) also yield only hindsight vis-a-vis the trials but underline the lack of credibility which the defence and petitioners claimed.

In that regard there must be a faint suspicion expressed in relation to the improvement, from the prosecution's point of view, in Burke's evidence between the first and second trials and his deposition before Brownrigg (54, 61, 96), as to his identification of the alleged murderers in the moments before the shot was fired.

The evidence of landlord Trant also improved between the trials (47, 59). It is remarkable too that he claimed that Ellis's life was not in danger for the previous three or four years (60) despite the general understanding that the police were patrolling the roads to protect him on those Thursdays (119).

One might note in passing that the performance of the police in Killahara/ Kilrush was questionable in the light of Sub-Constable Douglas's evidence in the Anne Brophy case (119). But Constable Arthur of Nenagh has to get credit on the double, both in relation to his firm action arising from Thomas Burke's chatter to driver Gleeson and Sub-Constable Kenny (94-5).

Was the Defence adequate?

The cross-examinations by Counsellors Rolleston and Johnstone, Rolleston's closing speech (62-6) and Johnstone's rearguard action on the approver-or-corroborator argument (68) are all impressive.

What must be questioned is their lack of initiative to pursue the forensics – why did they not visit the site, a prudent action for which there was local precedent in 1839. On that occasion a magistrate friend of the defence brought six 'respectable gentlemen' to visit the murder scene and performed a simple test. They undermined thereby the evidence of an eye witness whose general credibility had already been assailed by the defence counsel.[4] (There were certain similarities between that eye witness and Burke). The Crown then withdrew the case. The Ellis murder scene surely deserved to be inspected for the height and thickness of the hedge.

Three researchers did a test recently close to an anniversary of the murder. It was a bright, starry night without moonlight, equivalent to the conditions on 22 October 1858. Our conclusion was that faces could not be identified, contrary to Burke's claim (52). Silhouettes of one or two acquaintances probably could, but at somewhat more leisure than available to someone in his circumstances.

It is puzzling why the defence did not take an appeal on the point of law relating to Burke's eligibility as a corroborator. Can it be that they bet on acceptance by Lord Lieutenant Eglinton of the jury's recommendation to mercy? Did they think that a loss of an appeal would give added credence to Burke's evidence in the eyes of Eglinton and weaken the chances of his commuting the sentence? Is it possible that they were influenced in their inaction by the presence as Lord Chief Justice of the Queen's Bench, which was the court of appeal in criminal cases, of Baron Lefroy. At that stage he was eighty-two years of age and the survivor of a House of Commons debate two years previously on mooted removal from office. Baron Lefroy was also a landlord in North Tipperary, with a reputation of benevolence during the Great Famine but with a general anti-Emancipation and anti-liberal reputation from earlier days.[5]

Was Judge Keogh guilty

of outraging the 'decorum of the court' (111), having 'laid aside a calm and impartial air ... to assume the excited tones of the impassioned advocate' (104)?

On the one hand, he did brush aside the eavesdropper Sadleir's evidence (64). He did draw attention to Catherine's evidence, pointing out that 'it would displace the case of the Crown' and that of Burke 'if they could rely on it' (85). On the other hand, although he stated that Burke had behaved 'in a manner most discreditable' (55), he deemed him truthful at the trial as distinct from the inquest (71). He attached importance to the fact that William did not get up when called by the news of the murder – at its very best circumstantial evidence.

Keogh advised the first jury that there were untainted witnesses (55), and during his sentencing speech that there was sufficient proof without Spillane's evidence (72). He declared after the verdict that he had 'turned the evidence over and over in his mind and did not entertain a doubt' (70) and likewise told Larcom that he did not doubt the propriety of the jury's verdict (85).

In judging Keogh it is his worth as a judge of evidence rather than his integrity that comes into question on all those points. And it is his knowledge of law that comes under scrutiny in declaring that Burke was not an accomplice (67). As argued in the text (68) it is hard to understand why he did not state a case to the superior court for judgement on this point, unless it was that he was not aware of the import of the 1848 act enabling him to do so. To suspect so would stretch to the limit an argument that he was incompetent: he was both a practising barrister and an MP at that time.

In his favour he laid heavy stress on innocence until guilt was proved without a reasonable doubt (66), he gave an unusually long interval between sentence and date of execution (113), his notes from the trial were made available for the Cormacks' own petition, whether by his agency or by the Crown solicitors (79). He took the initiative in drawing the government's attention to the reasons for the jury's recommendation to mercy, together with an offer to obtain and forward the relevant information (76). He stood over his lack of doubts on the verdict by saying he did not know of any circumstance other than Catherine's alleged seduction to justify mercy (85), then responded beyond the call of duty, so to speak, by forwarding the Leahy-Cullen last throw (86).

An historian must conclude, in all fairness, that Keogh, deemed guilty of 'deadly treason' on the political front (109), was a soft target for the politicians of 1858 and particularly in 1910 when the names of Jones, Goold, Sadleir, Rock and Whiteside were forgotten.

WAS THE PETTY JURY GUILTY

of 'judicial murder' (128)? One has to leave aside all the polemic relating to a 'prejudiced, partisan, packed jury' (154, 77, 82, 100) in the light of the simple fact that three members were Roman Catholics and contributed to the unanimous twelve-man verdict. There is, of course, no justice in impugning the integrity of the other nine in the absence of specific charges of vested interest by individuals and/or proven examples of any sectarian or racist bias, as distinct from generalised attacks on the undoubtedly serious flaws in the selection system. It was unknown to the lore which has passed from generation to generation that they petitioned the Lord Lieutenant for the men's lives (78). As they pointed out, they were partly governed by the judge's instruction that Burke was not an approver. They also confirmed that they believed his evidence, again influenced by Judge Keogh (78). The trial jury did not know what we now know about Burke, arising from his statements to the car driver and police on his way to emigration and his subsequent unconvincing retraction.

Their verdict was delivered after an hour and a quarter's deliberation; one wonders had some or all been present in the courtroom during William's trial two days previously and therefore had the advantage of being over the course twice. Can it be that the experience of the first jury who had been unable to come to a decision after nineteen and a half hours, debarred from 'food, drink and fire',[6] was a subconscious influence greater than the judge's injunction as to 'benefit of the doubt' (67). If so, perhaps the verdict was cushioned for them by the recommendation to mercy. Or the words of a jurist-writer, drawing on a modern study, may be apposite: 'It must, however, be remembered, that, though there is a presumption of innocence upon which the rules of evidence are based, yet there is a natural tendency to assume that an accused person committed for trial after an examination before a magistrate is probably guilty'[7].

The folklore which recounted the Cormacks' story over the decades expanded with some myths. One of these was that all the members of the jury died of a throat disease, with the implication that Providence had exercised retribution. The death records of only three have been found and the causes of death were cirrhosis of the liver, a stroke, and a heart condition.

WAS THE LORD LIEUTENANT GUILTY

of having 'gratified the appetite of a bigoted, exterminating and ascendancy caste' (154), or had he 'spared no labour or time' before fulfilling his 'painful duty' (87)? It is difficult to understand why he went against the very appealing personal message of Archbishop Leahy (83) and the strong point that this was an unprecedented petition based on the public 'being satisfied beyond all doubt of the innocence of the Cormacks', backed by a hint that the 'real perpetrators' were known (82-3). The papers of Under Secretary Thomas A Larcom, deposited in the manuscript section of the National Library of Ireland, include several newspaper cuttings. This shows that he was aware of the public's dissatisfaction with the conviction.

It may be that the psyche of the chief governor of Ireland was not capable of comprehending the Irish countryside, except as regards the dangers to landlords and land agents. The same issue of the *Nenagh Guardian* as reported the trials listed the Lord Lieutenant's 'Household'/Viceregal 'Court': as well as seven administrative staff it included Gentlemen at Large, Gentlemen of the Bed Chamber, and eleven Aides-de-Camp.[8] To illustrate further the different lifestyles and mindsets of the governing and the governed, here is Attorney-General Whiteside telling the jury: 'in that house persons were in the habit of meeting and playing cards. I don't know whether or not this species of gambling is common in this county but ... persons used to assemble in this house and play for money'.[9]

After all that and leaving aside the law,

WERE THE CORMACKS GUILTY OR INNOCENT?

The points were well made by Rolleston of the unlikelihood of their engaging the likes of Spillane (63), and by the letter-writer M.M. and the Leahy petition that they had everything to lose if they were to kill Ellis (77, 81). But a dispassionate reviewer might have niggling doubts about what Sadleir overheard in Thurles bridewell (54, 62) – could it bear a malign interpretation? Likewise, the failure of William to leave his bed on being told of the murder (64, 71).

There is then the crucial matter of a motive. The section above in relation to the prosecution has recapitulated on Ellis's reputation for low morals. Any link between the rumoured seduction of Catherine, or indeed confirmation of the rumour, could only be proven by a baptismal record of a child with her as the mother, and with the name of Ellis entered as its father in the church register. No such record has been found in the records of Loughmore-Castleiny RC parish or surrounding parishes. In the baptismal record of children born out of wedlock in that era it is usual, rather than unusual, to find the father's name recorded also.

M.M.'s letter dismissed the rumour (77). In early August 1858 Dr Patrick Leahy, Archbishop of Cashel & Emly, while travelling on the train from Dublin to Thurles, engaged in a conversation about the Cormacks with a Mr E. M. Dunne of Mountrath. Ten days later, on 13 August, he saw fit to write the following letter to his travelling companion.

... I stated to you the impression in my mind to the effect that Ellis had seduced their sister – that was at the time the impression in my mind, derived from, I believe, well-founded rumour. I have since learned ... is most probably, if not certainly, no fact at all, but a suspicion.

In justice to the poor Female in question, who has the same right to her good name as the highest lady in the land, I feel bound to retract, what on the faith of rumour I stated to her prejudice, and further to request you will directly make known the retraction to any one to whom you may have chanced to communicate the material. ...[10]

That Ellis had indeed fathered a male Cormack child was a firm conviction in local lore up to quite recent times. The basis for the conviction was that a man known as Daniel Cormack, a tailor by trade, who lived in Templemore but moved around the area working with tailors, was the son of John Ellis and one of the Cormack girls.

This Daniel identified himself to John Walsh, Hon. Secretary of the organising committee, in Templemore on the day of the funeral in 1910 as 'the next of kin'.[11] He was born to the unmarried Anne/Nancy Cormack in Thurles workhouse in July 1859, nearly two years after Ellis's death. This was her second child as she had given birth to a daughter in September 1857 – seven weeks before the murder of John Ellis.

The father of her daughter is recorded in the church registers as Michael Roche. The text implies (60) that he was the Roche alleged by Spillane to have been an intended target of Daniel Cormack.

The father of Nancy's second child is recorded as Daniel Dwyer.[12] And to round out the story: Daniel Dwyer, a retired tailor, died in Thurles workhouse in 1932. His age on the record is 72 years, so differing by just a year from the 1859 birth date of Nancy Cormack's son.

An assessment of the probabilities of the case must take into account
• Judge Keogh's nightmare almost twenty years later, even allowing for a garbling of the exact words he used when recounted thirty-four years later again in 1910 (155);
• their own protestations of innocence, on the scaffold, whatever about those in the courtroom, accentuated by the moving account by the chaplain of Daniel's attitude (90-1);
• their solicitor Edward Dwyer's confirmation that they did not confess guilt but persisted in a 'most pathetic and solemn assurance of their innocence' (114);
• again, the impressive list of signatories to the Leahy memorial and the vehemence of their final paragraphs (82-3).
• Inspector Price's relay in 1910 of the local opinion that a man named Gleeson confessed at the time and 'on his death bed in America' (140).

There are now the following post scripts:
• Mother Mary Cassidy of the Sisters of Mercy, the new tenants of the county gaol, wrote in *Molua* in 1953:

Some twelve years previous to this [1910] demonstration [i.e. in 1898], an American priest – Rev. W. Coonan, Bradford, Pa., U.S. called at the Convent and asked to see the [Cormacks'] grave. 'I think', he said, 'that I gave the last absolution to the real murderer. He had always been wandering about, got his foot frost-bitten, and was unable to proceed further'. It is understood that he was unable to speak when the priest arrived, but those who knew him always said it was he committed the deed, and that he was actually in Nenagh the day of the execution. He was deeply penitent, the unhappy man, and it is said that he wanted to give himself up that day to save them, but was told that it would avail them nothing.

• a comment by Rev. Walter Skehan, P.P., Loughmore-Castleiny added to his transcript of the contents of the Larcom papers: 'The actual murderer, according to local lore, was a man named Gleeson, grand-uncle of Bridie Gleeson of Kilkillahara (living 1971).'

• a statement in the *Nenagh News* issue of 14 May 1910: 'It is only right to say that the man who murdered Ellis was one William Gleeson, an evicted tenant, who died some time ago in New York.'

Finally, we should spare a thought for the cause of it all, John Ellis, flawed character though he was, and for his grief-stricken family (48).

NOTES

1   Denis G. Marnane, *Land & Violence in West Tipperary* (Tipperary 1985), pp. 56, 58.

2   *Letters of a Tipperary Man to the Earl of Derby*, (Liverpool 1861). The open letters were written over a period in 1859 and 1860 and published in the *Liverpool Mercury* newspaper.

3   V.T.H. Delany, *Christopher Palles*, p. 30.

4   Daniel Grace, 'The Murder of James Meara' in *Cloughjordan Heritage*, No. 3 1992, pp. 6-11.

5   Delany, cited above, p. 29; Grace, *Portrait of a Parish*, pp. 50, 100: Baron Thomas L. Lefroy owned the 874 acres of Knigh townland near Nenagh; Murphy, *Two Tipperarys*, pp. 46-7n.

6   Kenny's *Outlines*, p. 616, n 2. It was only in 1870 that it became permissible for a jury to have 'reasonable refreshments'.

7   ditto, p. 636.

8   *NG*, 17 Mar 1858.

9   *LR & TV*, 16 Mar 1858.

10 NLI, Larcom Papers MS 7636; copy in Cormack file County Library, Thurles.

11 Verbal account to the author by the late Paul Walsh, Templemore, son of John Walsh.

12 Thurles RC parish records. Very Rev. Maurice Dooley, P.P., Loughmore-Castleiny, drew my attention to the Roche and Dwyer entries.

Who were the Cormacks?

The Roman Catholic registers for Loughmore-Castleiny parish show three Cormack couples, with Killahara as their address, parenting children between 1814 and 1838. The table below shows the three of them and their children. As already stated, none of the couples had the combination of a William, Daniel, Catherine and Anne/Nancy – the names mentioned in the trial as comprising the family at the centre of attention.

Michael Cormack married Catherine Maher in 1813		John Cormack married Judith Doherty in 1822		James Cormack married Catherine Maher in 1832	
Children	**Year born**	**Children**	**Year born**	**Children**	**Year born**
Thomas	1814	William	1823 (died)	**Catherine**	**1833**
John	1815	James	1824	Mary	1835
Mary	1819	Mary	1825	**William**	**1837**
Michael	1821	Charles	1827	**Anne/Nancy**	**1841**
William	**1824**	**William**	**1828**	James	1844
Anne	**1828**	John	1830		
Daniel	**1831**	Judith	1832		
Patt	1835	**Catherine & Nancy**	**1834**		
		Ellen	1835		
		Bridget	1838		

Michael and Catherine (née Maher) Cormack had a William baptised in 1824, so older by eight years than the stated age (26) of the executed William. They had no daughter Catherine. There is an entry in the register for a Daniel baptised in 1831. Unfortunately, the priest did not enter the father's first name but as the mother's name was Catherine Maher the father was probably the above Michael. This Daniel would be 27 in 1858 as against 23 for the executed Daniel. Their daughter Anne would be 43 in 1875, as against the age of 40 given for the death of the executed men's sister of that name.

John and Judith (née Doherty) Cormacks' son William is four years older than the age (26) given in official documents for the William executed. The birth date of twins Catherine and Nancy tallies with the age on the 1875 official death certificate of the executed men's sister, Nancy. However, John and Judith had no child named Daniel – at least no baptismal record of a Daniel having those parents has been found in the RC baptismal records of

Loughmore-Castleiny or of any of the surrounding parishes.[1]

Patrick Joseph Ryan, Oldbawn Cottage, Loughmore, local historian, who wrote the story of the Cormack Brothers in the publication, *An Droichead*,[2] is of the opinion that this is the family in question and that the name Ellen (1835) was inadvertently entered in the register instead of Daniel – there were three other baptisms entered for the same date and one of them is an Ellen McGrath. Very Rev. Maurice Dooley, P.P., has confirmed that the entry in the original register is for an Ellen Cormack.

He also points out that there are two lots of bulk entries in the register for the year 1832. A total of 43 were entered for January and 15 for June, with no individual baptismal dates. The probable explanation for this may be the ill-health of the parish priest, as he died in December 1832. This increases the likelihood of some names having been missed out altogether.

If one accepts that the Cormacks' mother was Doherty, the Maher connection has to originate with John Cormack or Judy Doherty's mother. An exploration of the records suggests that this John Cormack was of the family of William and Mary née Healy. Alas, there is no Doherty-Maher combination parenting children who, agewise, could be Judith's family.

James Cormack and Catherine Maher married in February 1832. This rules out the Daniel of 1831, whose father's Christian name is omitted, being their child as that baptismal entry is the standard type used for married couples, i.e. the father's name entered first. The record for children born out of wedlock usually has the mother's name entered first.

However, the time lapse between James and Catherine's marriage and the birth of their first recorded child – Catherine in November 1833 – is sufficient for them to have had an earlier child. One could conjecture that a son, Daniel, was born in that period but not entered in the register for the reasons outlined above. This would make him 25 or 26 years in 1858, as against the age of 23 years given in the official documents for the Daniel executed. This couple's William is 21 years in 1858 as against age 26 given for the executed William.

One is presented here with three difficulties: (a) the absence of a Daniel; (b) the difference between their William's age and that of the executed man; and (c) their Anne being six years younger than the Anne/Nancy who died in 1875 and who has been identified with reasonable certainty as the sister of the executed men.

That identification emanated from Francis Bannon, a teacher in Kilcummin/Kilcommon National School, near Rearcross, Thurles, and appeared in the *Nenagh News* of 4 December 1909 arising from a news item on the intended re-burial.

In Mar 1875 I was elected to the position of teacher in the Poor Law Union of Thurles and I held the position until Mar 1877. When I was there [in the workhouse] a woman named Nancy Cormack was a helper in the store. One of her chief duties was to help in the distribution of the meals, including the luncheons for the school children. I very soon was informed that she was the sister of the ill-fated Cormacks. Though I was very young and thoughtless at the time, she at once had my deep sympathy. My opportunities for showing her little kindnesses were very few and almost inappreciable. But somehow she seemed to know how I felt for her. She never came over with the boys' lunches but that I had a few minutes chat with her and I always chose a cheerful subject. But there was always a sad expression in her countenance which showed that there was a memory in her 'rooted sorrow'. She died while I was there and the only token of respect I could show her remains was to get a special coffin made for her and to follow it to the grave.

The rest of my letter is strange but true. The railway line passes immediately at the back of the Workhouse and Mr Walsh, the Master, who knew her in the institution for a considerable time, told me that the train carrying the assizes judge to Nenagh never passed but she got a weakness, remained unconscious for some time and appeared dazed for the rest of the day, performing any light duties allotted to her mechanically and unwilling to speak or be spoken to.

The only pointer to the probable location of the Cormacks' house in Killahara comes from the map Samuel Cooke compiled shortly after the murder (p. 27). An examination of the Primary Valuation Books, House Books, Lists and corresponding maps, and the Thurles Poor Law Union rate books,[3] provide no information which could be linked to the buildings identified by Cooke. While a John Cormack and a James Cormack appear in the House Books for Killahara townland,[4] they are not referenced to maps.

Finally, the manuscript section of the National Library has a collection of papers from the Trant estate, Dovea. The collection includes records of rent and wages, day book, farm accounts and diaries.[5] While these are a most valuable cache of documents they yield nothing on the Cormacks, apart from the fact that Trant bought potatoes from a William Cormack in 1846 and rented grazing for a cow to a Daniel in 1847. No names appear in the wages record, merely 'Kilrush labourers a/c' and 'Dovea labourers a/c'. Phil Maher, the smith, did regular work for Trant before and after the Ellis murder and execution of the Cormacks.

WHAT HAPPENED TO CATHERINE?

In May 1859 the *Limerick Reporter & Tipperary Vindicator* announced that a testimonial was being organised to 'enable the afflicted sisters of the ill-fated brothers Cormack to emigrate to America, to a still-surviving brother and sister that have for some time settled there'. It was intended that they would travel from Galway on the *Prince Albert* to New York 'immediately'. The advertisement carried a list of subscribers; their donations – mostly £1 or 10 shillings – came to £14.

The list, headed by Archbishop Patrick Leahy, included Edward Dwyer, solicitor, clergy from parishes around Thurles, and the *LR & TV*'s proprietor-editor, Maurice Lenihan. Rev. W. Wall, P.P., Thurles, was the Treasurer.[6]

It would appear that Catherine did travel for no trace has been found of her death record, nor does she appear in the 1901 census for Tipperary North.[7] No details as to her fate are preserved in local lore.

The fact that James Maher, thought to have been their first cousin, was one of the next-of-kin on whose behalf the exhumation request was made in 1910, pointed towards the probability of a Cormack-Maher combination of parents. This influenced opting on page 10 for James Cormack and Catherine Maher as the likely parents. However, that conclusion is thwarted to some extent by the discovery at a late stage in research that the Cormack brothers had another brother and sister America. While this couple had a daughter Mary born in 1835, their other son, if he was alive, would only be 15-years-old in 1859.

It is extraordinary that the names of William and Daniel Cormacks' parents, and other family details, were not ascertained from their cousins, Thomas Cormack, Killahara, and James Maher, Leugh, Thurles, and published in 1910. James, who was at their trial, execution, exhumation and re-burial, was in his mid-eighties when he died in 1914.

NOTES

1   Parish records indexing project, Thurles, 1984.
2   Vol. vi, no.s 6, 7 (1985), edited and published by Jim and Biddy Condon, Thurles.
3   Valuation office, Dublin, Primary/Griffith's Valuation maps, sheets 35 & 41. Unfortunately, the location of houses and small portions of land in Killahara townland, of which John Trant was the landlord, are not individually marked. An extensive acreage marked '1' embraces occupiers '1a' to '1m' on the printed list.
4   NLI, House Books, Loughmore West and Kilrush EDs; Co. Library, poor law rate books for the same EDs.
5   NLI, Trant Papers MSS 1607, 1757, 1759-61, 2566-2573.
6   *LR & TV*, 31 May, 3, 7, 10 June 1859.
7   TNFH Research Centre, index to death and gravestone records and 1901 census.

The Leahy Petition Signatories

John Cooney, P.P., Loughmore
David L. Cambie
William Ryan
Thomas Mullany P.P., Drom
John Cullen
James Ryan
James McNamara, OSA
Daniel K Lanigan, P.P., Kilcummin
Michael Harney
Benjamin Hayes
Walter Cantwell, P.P., Cashel
Stokes & Hayes, Thurles
Michl Kenny, Thurles
Richd Sutcliffe, Thurles
Richard Lalor Cambie
Daniel Maher
William Kirwan, Solicitor
Sol Lalor Cambie, J.P.
John Bourke, P.P., Moycarkey
Michl Mulany, Beakstown
William Ryan
William Wall P.P. Thurles
Thomas Molony
Wm Molony
Anthony Dwyer, Merchant Thurles
Michael Banon, P.P., Moyne
John Kenny, Thurles
John Finn
Patrick Davy, Thurles
Thomas Delany, Thurles
John Bergin
Thomas Ryan
William Poe
John Stapleton
Michael Dwyer
Edmond Cass

Bryan Haidon
Michael Leahy
John Quirke
John J. Morkan
John Leatham
Michael Leatham
Kate Maher
Kate Molony
Patrick O'Brien
William Creagh
Thomas Conway
Michael Kenny
John Power
Alexander McDonnell
William Clear
John Quinlisk
Michael Gleeson
Pat Dunn
Robert Wood, Apothocary
James Wood
John Coughlan
Richard Hayes
John Maunsell
P. Maher
Pierse Walsh
John Toomey
Daniel O'Leary
Thomas Day
?Kevin Molony
Patrick McKeough
Thomas Ryan
James Crotty
Thomas Dolan
John Fanning
John Sheehan
Hugh Shelly

Edmund Ryan
Thomas Cahill
Timothy Ryan
James Ryan
Edward Holohan
Martin Keogh
William Boyton
William Ryan
James Walsh
Mary Harney
Edmond Hayes
John Darmody
John Ryan
Richard Donnelly, Thurles
William O'Shea
John Quirk
William Hickey
Patrick Dwyer
John Ryan
John O'Brien
Michael Brien
John Darmody
Pat Walshe
Patrick Cormack
James Smee
Patrick Darmody
Michael Purcell
Cornelious McNamara
Timothy Kearin
Martin Connors
Patrick McGrath
James D'Acre
Patt McGarry
John Hughes
John Hamilton

James H. Poe, Rector, Nenagh
Daniel McKeogh, Surgeon
Michael Meagher
John F Magrath, Solicitor

William Carey, Solicitor, Nenagh
T. Cleary, C.C., Nenagh
– Macklin, TC, Nenagh
Daniel O'Meara, Merchant, Nenagh
James Connell, Nenagh
Peter B. Cooke, Nenagh
Daniel Kennedy, Ballahane
James Spain, Surgeon, Nenagh
Denis Dwyer, Merchant, Nenagh
John Dwyer, Nenagh
Daniel Clancy, Merchant, Nenagh
Michael Dwyer
John Donoghoe, Merchant, Nenagh
Michael John Cahalan MRCPI,
    Nenagh
Joseph MaGrath, P.P., Kilcommin
Anthony Nolan, TC, Nenagh
Ellen Jones, Nenagh
Patrick O'Brien, Nenagh
John Power
Thomas O'Brien, Nenagh
James Hanly, Merchant, Nenagh
William Dillon, Tyone, Nenagh
Patrick O'Leary, Merchant
Patrick McGrath, RCC, Silvermines
James O'Brien, TC, Merchant
Patk O'Brien, Merchant, Nenagh
Martin Corbett, TC, Merchant
    Nenagh
Michael Dunne, Nenagh
Andrew Murphy, Nenagh
Patrick Toohy, Nenagh
Patrick Cleary, TC, Nenagh
John Pine, Merchant, Nenagh
John Tumpane, Merchant, Nenagh
Patrick McGrath, Nenagh
Jim Maher, Nenagh
Rody Meara, Nenagh
Fanny Nolan, Nenagh
Thomas Pine, JP, Nenagh
Edwd Gleeson, Merchant Nenagh

Michael Flannery, Nenagh
Jeremiah Starr, Nenagh
Michael Cleary, Nenagh
John Pine, Nenagh
Edwd Pine, Merchant, Nenagh
John Scanlan, P.P., Nenagh
M Gleeson, TC
Pat Cahalan
Bryan Considine
M. Nihan, Nenagh
Patk Shannon, C.C.
Robert McCreedy
John Talbot, Nenagh
Margaret Flannery
Henry Downs, Nenagh
John Dwyer, Killnafinch
Brien Jones, Nenagh
James Hogan, Mercht, Nenagh
John Carroll, Hotel Keeper
Martin Walsh, Nenagh
William Dwyer , Nenagh
Philip Slattery, Nenagh
James Gleeson, Nenagh
Catherine Boland, Nenagh
John Brindly, Ballivan
Philip McGrath, Merchant, Nenagh
Ellen Ryan, Nenagh
John Berkery, Nenagh
Thomas Reddin, Mercht, Nenagh
Michael Grady, Nenagh
Michael Molamphy, Nenagh
Jno Hill, Nenagh
Mary MaGrath, Nenagh
Daniel Helebert, PLG, Castletown
John Moylan, Nenagh
Martin Hogan, Faunlough
Darby Grace, Capadine
James Grace, Blain
Martin Gason, Annbrook
John D O'Ryan, Cloghonan,
    PLG & DC Nenagh Union

Michael Burke, P.P., Clonmel
David Clancy, Mayor of Clonmel
John Baldwan, RCC, St Mary's
Edw Phelan, JP
Cornelius Darmody
James & Mrs Shee, ?Greenane,
    Tipperary
James ?Kitt, Manager Nat Bank
    Clonmel
J. Hackett, JP, Alderman,
Wm Hackett, AB, Barrister at Law
Jno W. Dowsley
Wm Keating, TC, Merchant
– Dick, TC
Charles Keeffe, Merchant
Morgan Luther, Merchant
Martin Kennedy, Merchant
Robt F Morgan, Main Street,
    Clonmel
Michl Guiny, Mercht, Clonmel
William Ryan, Solr
John Luther, JP
Ben Wright, Clonmel
J. P. Leader, Draper
Laur McGrath
Michl O'Riordan
Augustine Devine, Merchant
Thomas Daniel
James –, TC
Jno Ryan
John Forde, Main St
Bryan Williams & Co.
Edwd Stokes
W. Burke
John Luther, Town Clerk
A. S. Cooke
Matthew Scully, Apothecary
Samuel Holmes
John Morrissey
Wm Hopkins
John Moran

John Thornton
Denis Cooney
Thomas O'Shaughnessy, Merchant,
  Clonmel
Wm Sparrow, Clonmel
John Spackman, Clonmel
William Skehan, Clonmel
John Hogan, Clonmel
William Lonergan
J. Davy, Clonmel
James Newell
Lorian Brett
Wm Pollard
H. Jones
D. Garratt
Patrick Armstrong
John Armstrong
Patrick Hanigan
Thomas Ward
Mathew Scanlan
James Shea
P. Tobin, Dublin
Michl P. Tobin , Clonmel
A. McDonald, Barrister at Law
John O'Donnell
Wm Cahill
Philip Power
John D. Roper, Surgeon
John Casey
J. M. Dann
Robert Pelliseir
Patrick Hayes, Merchant, Clonmel
Thomas Hill, Clonmel

John Cleary
Jeremiah Murphy
John Walsh
Patt Ryan
Francis Moore
William Wright
Luther Daneil
Wright & Ryan
William Hudson
D. Corcoran, TC
Thomas Hannigan
Patrick O Mahony
John Maher
William Massey
John Thornton
David Thornton
Thos H–
John Murphy
Patrick O'Neill
Benjamin Murphy, Brewer
William Lanphier
Henry Massey
John Cleary
James Moloney
Thomas Brinkley
Patrick Casey, TC
James Cleary, TC
James Hogan
D.A. Higgins, Alderman
J. A. O'Neill
Thomas Cantwell, TC
Edward Cantwell, TC
Patrick Fennely, Alderman

The Loughmore West Signatories

All signatories, apart from Cooke, lived in Loughmore West parish or Kilrush townland.
X denotes the signatory's mark due to inability to write

John Cooney, P.P.

KILKILLAHARA
William Connell
Patrick McGrath
Thomas Eagan
Patrick Fogarty
Daniel Morrissey
Patrick Ryan X
Timothy Geehan
Thomas Egan

CARRIG(LOUGHMORE)
Walter Bourke
James Brennan X
Patrick Ryan, Carrig X
Ellen Stapleton,widow X
Catherine Tuohy, widow

KILRUSH
Sam Cooke, PLG,
  Kilrush ED
Michael Maher X
Michael Glennon X
James Halpin X
Bridget Bourke,
  widow X
John Gleeson
Mary Darmody X
Richard Maher X
John Maher X
Pat O'Shea X
Philip Kerwick X
Thomas Maher X
William Dee
Thomas Reilly X
John Dee X
James Ryan X

Andrew Kirwan X
William Gleeson X
Robin Ryan X
Tim Ryan X
John Fogarty
James Burke X
James Maher

RUCKER/ROCKER
Thomas Russell
Michael Cahill X
Thomas Comerford
Thomas Comerford Snr

CASTLEQUARTER
John Maher
Edmond McGrath
Richard Bourke X
Michael Cahill X

BALLYBRISTA/BRISTY
Patrick Brien X
Batt Gleeson, X
Michael Ryan
Lawrence Gleeson
Patrick Maher X

LOUGHKILL/LAGHILE
John Cormick,
John Mara
Martin Carrol
Michael Ryan

LISHEENATAGGART
Michael Kennedy,
William Maher X
John Finn
Andy Long

Johana Cleary X
William Tuohy X
William Fogarty
Thomas Fogarty
Timothy Fogarty

WHITEFIELD
Pat Maguire X
John Ormond
Bridget Harney, widow
James Ryan
William Fogarty X

KILLAHARA
John Cleary X
Michael Carroll
Andrew Nolan X

CLONDOTY
Con Carroll
William Fanning

TINVOHER
John Woodlock X
Cath Cormick, widow X
Daniel Keogh
Patrick Carrol
John Cahill
Patrick Fogarty X
John Londergan
Michael Purcel
James Ryan
Patt Keogh
Lant Carroll
Michael Kavanagh
Patrick Cahill X
John Henesey

Anonymous

The Ballad of the Cormack Brothers

All you true-born Irishmen I hope you lend an ear
And hear a true narration of those lines I have penned down here,
Just leave awhile your cares and toil and then a memorial we will raise
To the memory of the Cormack boys who were hanged in Nenagh Gaol.

It was in the year of '57, all in the troubled times,
When cruel eviction was spreading through our isle;
Bad landlords and their agents were the rulers of our land,
It was then that Ellis was shot down – all by an unknown hand.

When the news spread round Killahara that the Agent he was shot,
The Police were soon informed and assembled on the spot;
They searched each field and garden, every house and every shed,
Until they came to the Cormacks' house, where those two lads were in bed.

They accused those boys of murder from information they had got,
From a Coachman who was passing at the time Ellis was shot;
They said that they were innocent, but it was of no avail,
They were handcuffed and made prisoners of and conveyed to the County Gaol.

At the Spring Assizes those two boys stood trial in Nenagh Town,
And by a packed jury they both were guilty found;
The Judge addressed the prisoners and he asked what they had to say,
Before he signed their executions for the 11th day of May.

'It was in Killahara we were reared, between Thurles and Templemore,
Well known to all the inhabitants round the parish of Loughmore;
We are innocent of shooting Ellis as the child in its cradle do lie,
And we cannot see, for another man's deed, why we're both condemned to die?'

On the 11th of May in '58 the hanging it took place,
And by a holy Pastor they were both reconciled to grace;
Such thunder, rain and lightning has not been witnessed since,
As the Lord above sent down from Heaven as a token of their innocence.

Now to conclude and to finish, let all good Christians pray
For the Cormack brothers, who are mouldering in the clay;
May the Lord have mercy on their souls, for alas they are no more;
May their souls reside in heaven and their bodies in Loughmore.